OWLS

Floyd Scholz

Photographs by Tad Merrick

STACKPOLE
BOOKS

Published by
STACKPOLE BOOKS
5067 Ritter Road
Mechanicsburg, PA 17055
www.stackpolebooks.com

Printed in China

10 9 8 7 6 5 4 3

First edition

Photographs by Tad Merrick (unless otherwise credited)
Species profile drawings by Floyd Scholz
Species head portraits by Reed A. Prescott III

Library of Congress Cataloging-in-Publication Data

Scholz, Floyd.
    Owls : an artist's guide to understanding owls / Floyd Scholz.—1st ed.
        p.   cm.
    Includes bibliographical references (p.   ).
    ISBN 0-8117-1021-1
    1. Owls. 2. Owls in art. I. Title.

QL696.S83 S355 2001
598.9'7—dc21   00-067025
ISBN 978-0-8117-1021-3

For David, Alex, Ramon Antonio, and Ana Luisa—
four little people who have given me
a new perspective on life and on love

In memoriam
Floyd Scholz, Sr.
1930–1994
I am who I am because of you

CONTENTS

NON-EARED OWLS (Continued)
Northern Spotted Owl
Northern Hawk Owl
Boreal Owl
Snowy Owl
Great Gray Owl

Project 1 "FOREST GLOW"
Project 2 "MOONLIGHT OBSERVER"

THE FAR SIDE

By GARY LARSON

ACKNOWLEDGMENTS

WRITING A BOOK IS LIKE TAKING A JOURNEY. YOU cross paths with many people along the way whom without your expedition could not possibly succeed. I would like to deeply thank the following loved ones and friends, new and old, who have added so much to my trip.

To my beautiful wife, Beatriz, for her help and wisdom and for unselfishly giving me the time I needed to do it right. And to my mother, Muriel, whose big heart and optimism are an inspiration to all who know and love her. I'm blessed to share my life with Ramon and Evelyn, David and Helenia, Bea and Eli. To Nancy Merrill for her hard work, friendship, vision, and ideas. *A mi familia Venezolana por su apoyo.* To Tony Peters, my friend and right-hand man. To Tad Merrick, the greatest friend and associate anyone could hope for and, of course, a photographer extraordinaire. To Reed Prescott for contributing great art. With love to Drs. Myron, Karin, and Sosha Yanoff who, from the beginning, helped make it all happen. To Auntie Donna, Laura, and Sal for always being there. To my dear friends Guy Coheleach, Steve North, Frank McMahon, Vern and Karolyn Hesketh, Dick and Dorothy Robson, Mike Cox, and the staff at the Vermont Raptor Center. To the Redington family—Rick, Julie, Maya, and Benjamin. Also to Ron Austing, Robert Taylor, Gary Larson, Melissa Irons and the staff at Far Works, Inc., and Bob and Kay Jones. And to the amazing Cathy Hart.

A very special thank you goes to Jonathan and Susan Wood and to Joseph and Dalel for the great dinner and great birds at the Raptor Project in Roxbury, New York, and to my friends Bob and Sam Fox at Wild at Heart in Cave Creek, Arizona, for opening their doors to Frank and me and sharing their time and enthusiasm.

To my editors, Mark Allison and Amy Hixon, for their hard work, and to Judith Schnell for owl-like patience and belief in this project. To Donna Pope, Tracy Patterson, Adrian Fleming, Shirley Lutz, and the wonderful people at Stackpole Books. And to Emma Patterson. Special thanks to my friend Mary Suggett and the staff at Andrews, McMeel Universal for opening a door. To Carole Precious, Ernie Muehlmatt, El Arnold, and Peter and Margie Stern for their friendship; Shane and Anna Scholz; my friend Paul Reed Smith, who is always an inspiration; Brother Joe Schenkman (the Skankdude); Charley and Sally Shelley for their undying enthusiasm and friendship, Ron and Nancy Walborn, Ben and Anne Bailar for acquiring my first pair of owls, and Dr. Cary Schwartz for his friendship and good humor; Steve and Robbie, Jimmy, Donna, Amelia, Avery and James Disabito, Rani Arbo, Scott Kessel, Andrew Kinsey, and Dave Dick for sharing their gifts of music and friendship; my good friend and comrade in arms Jim Hahn of Jaymes Co.; and, last but not least, all my friends old and new who have come up to Hancock, Vermont, and carved with me at the Vermont Raptor Academy. We live to carve and carve to live!

Floyd Scholz
Hancock, Vermont

Bizarro

by Dan Piraro

FOREWORD

As a painter whose favorite subjects are the predators, I started my career in what seems like the Dark Ages. To acquire information about our subjects, most of us had to rely on roadkills and long-distance vision, binoculars being a rare luxury. We built "swipe files" of very poor quality black-and-white photos from magazines, newspapers, books, and, in my case, primitive but vibrant sketches done in zoos and museums. There is, of course, no substitute for firsthand field experience. Whether sketching or just gazing and absorbing wildlife in its natural state, it is absolutely necessary to use real life as a reference for judging whether your photos are useful. I also trapped wild birds and borrowed study skins from the American Museum of Natural History. With the advent of color photography, the quality of reference material increased enormously.

As I mentioned in Floyd Scholz's previous book, *Birds of Prey,* all artists must rely on some sort of source material. That compilation of high-quality photos is an artist's dream come true for any novice or veteran interested in rendering the birds of prey. Likewise, this book on owls is the most comprehensive visual guide on these nocturnal hunters ever published. For anyone who works with owls, whether in two or three dimensions, this is an awesome collection of information and photographs on these winged predators.

Acquiring the material must have been a tremendous effort. The book is filled with informative text and over 700 clear photos and drawings of these magnificent creatures. It is a must for any artist, carver, ornithologist, or just plain nature watcher. *Owls* will join *Birds of Prey* as a standard in the nature library. How fortunate we all are for Floyd Scholz's efforts.

Guy Coheleach
Bernardsville, New Jersey

A wise old owl sat in an oak
and the more he sat, the less he spoke,
and the less he spoke, the more he heard,
Why can't we all be like that wise old bird?

—Early American rhyme, anonymous

THE ALLURE OF OWLS

WOWL WAS THE WORD SOFTLY SAID BY MY TWO-year-old granddaughter, Alexandra, as she pointed to a stuffed snowy owl standing guard in my studio.

"No, my little angel," I replied, "that's an owl. O-W-E-L-L."

She looked again. "Wowl!" she repeated confidently, then continued her task of exploring the room.

Months later, while researching the natural history of owls for this book, it occurred to me that perhaps Alexandra had it right. As I discovered the details of the behavior, evolution, and anatomy of this mysterious family of birds, I became convinced that the word *wow* belonged in there somewhere.

Owls are amazing creatures. Their physical and behavioral characteristics have been fine-tuned over millions of years to enable them not just to survive but to flourish in a worldwide niche unattainable by any other creature. At least one member of the owl family currently inhabits every continent on earth except Antarctica. The barn owl, which has benefited the most from the spread of human society, can be called a truly cosmopolitan species; it is found throughout the world.

If we were to wander back to the earliest days of human existence, we would be hard-pressed to find any animal—finned, furred, feathered, or otherwise—that has had such an emotional impact on human society as has the owl. Throughout history, owls have been both feared and revered. Certain peoples associated the birds with darkness, evil, and death; others looked on them as omens of wisdom, power, and good luck. Images of owl-like birds have been discovered on cave walls decorated thousands of years before recorded history, perhaps by shamans of ancient clans bewitched by the piercing shrieks and mournful hoots heard in the darkness beyond the glowing embers of a warm fire.

Millions of years of evolution have created a family of predators so good at what they do that even in today's high-tech world we still stand in awe of the owl. As a professional bird carver, I could be kept busy year-round honoring commissions to carve owls. At any given time, I have several standing orders for owls, from tiny saw-whet owls to powerful great horned owls.

Why are we so fascinated by owls? Part of the reason is probably because the birds often prefer the same types of surroundings we do. From an owl's perspective, where there are humans, there will be food, especially rats and mice that thrive on our leftovers. Owls also possess a number of humanlike characteristics—large, round heads; big, forward-facing eyes; an erect posture; and an ability to make a startling variety of vocalizations—that make them unlike most other animals.

I am certain that the ghosts inhabiting many a haunted house were nothing more than mom and dad barn owls bringing home groceries to a hungry family. Consider this scenario. You're walking past an old, dilapidated house on a cold and gloomy evening when from somewhere inside the building you hear a blood-curdling scream and a trailing, wailing moan. Your pulse begins to race. You hear a variety of creaks, snaps, and rattles. Then you see something floating behind the shattered glass of a second-story window—something otherworldly, deathly white, and completely silent. In no mood to investigate further, you turn tail and run.

It is likely that you have just come across a barn owl raising a brood in a suitable shelter. The birds have soft, silvery white underwings and bodies and a quiet, floating, undulating flight. Their vocalizations range from deep, snoring hisses and high-pitched shrieks to a variety of chainlike snaps and rattles. A bioluminescent fungus sometimes forms on the underside of a barn owl's wings, making the bird actually glow in the dark.

It's easy to see how an impressionistic and superstitious mind could be fooled. And it's easy to see how watching an owl can make anyone say "wowl!"

What Is an Owl?

owl \oul\ *noun : any of an order (Strigiformes) of night birds of prey found throughout the world, distinguished by a large, flat face, eyes surrounded by stiff feathered disks, a short, hooked beak, feathered legs with sharp talons, and soft plumage which permits noiseless flight*

stealth \stelth\ *noun : secret, furtive, or artfully sly action or behavior*

OWLS BELONG TO ONE OF TWO FAMILIES, TYTONIDAE or Strigidae, both of which ornithologists place in the taxonomic order Strigiformes. DNA analysis has revealed that owls are closely related to the Cuculiformes (the cuckoos) and the Caprimulgiformes (which include whip-poor-wills, nightjars, nighthawks, oil birds, and potoos). The relationship between these birds is based on physical appearance. They all have evolved certain characteristics that enable them to exploit a particular place in the natural order: They all possess the ability to overtake prey in low-light situations or near total darkness.

Until very recently, owls were thought to be closely related to eagles, hawks, and falcons. These birds collectively were called birds of prey. The only real difference, aside from outward appearances, was thought to be that owls hunted at night and the others hunted during the day. This classification, based on the similarity of prey items and tools used to survive, as well as on shared habitats, seemed to make sense, but when the evolutionary paths and basic physiology of the two groups were compared, striking differences became obvious.

SIZE

A trait that many owls share with hawks and other daytime predatory birds is a size and weight difference between the sexes, known as sexual dimorphism. Most female hawks and owls are considerably larger and heavier than the males. This difference is most evident in larger owls, which feed chiefly on vertebrate prey (large reptiles, mammals, and other birds), and is less obvious among the smaller owls. The exception to the rule is the terrestrial burrowing owl, in which the male of the species is larger and heavier than the female.

Experts have yet to establish a definitive reason for this size disparity, but many theories have been put forth. Some scientists believe that a larger female is better able to defend a nest or incubate a clutch of eggs. Others believe that the size disparity allows a pair of owls to exploit a wider ranger of food sources. No one knows for sure. I for one find it comforting that despite all our miracle technologies, we still don't have all the answers. Chalk one up for the birds.

VISION

Probably no other physical feature better distinguishes owls from other predatory birds than do their hypnotic, luminous eyes. For the record, in an environment completely devoid of light, owls cannot see any better than humans. Of course, even on the blackest of nights, a condition of total darkness almost never occurs. What sets the owl's eyes apart is their ability to amplify even the faintest light many times. This ability gives owls an almost supernatural ability to see in the dark, when most other animals cannot see a thing.

It has been surmised that the trade-off for possessing such powerful nighttime vision is the deterioration of daylight vision. This is absolutely not true. It is now widely believed that owls can see just as well as, if not better than, most other birds during daylight.

The eye's purpose is to gather light and convert it into an electrical message that is sent to the brain via the optic nerve. As light enters the eye, it is magnified many times by the bulbous outer cornea before traveling through the pupil into the eye's interior. Surrounding the pupil is a colored ring called the iris, which in the vast majority of owl species is either yellow or orange. The iris is a highly specialized diaphragm that expands and contracts to control the size of the pupil and, as a result, the amount of light that reaches the inner eye. In extreme bright-light conditions, such as during a sunny winter day with snow on the ground, the pupil contracts to a mere pinpoint in size. As the surroundings darken, the pupil enlarges, and less of the colored iris is visible.

Once light passes through the pupil, it is magnified a second time and focused through a thick, flat, transparent lens. This lens is controlled by tiny muscles that direct the incoming light onto the eye's extremely sensitive retina, located on the back wall of the eyeball, where it is converted into electrical impulses. The range of visual power of any animal depends on the manner in which light waves fall on the retina.

Among vertebrates, the retina contains two types of photosensitive receptors, called rods and cones because of their shapes. Cones are stimulated by higher light levels; rods are stimulated by softer or lower light. The eyes of creatures that hunt during daylight hours have many more cones than rods. In the case of hawks,

Opposite page: Perched up high and surveying his frigid domain, this adult great gray owl is an impressive sight in the great north woods. RON AUSTING

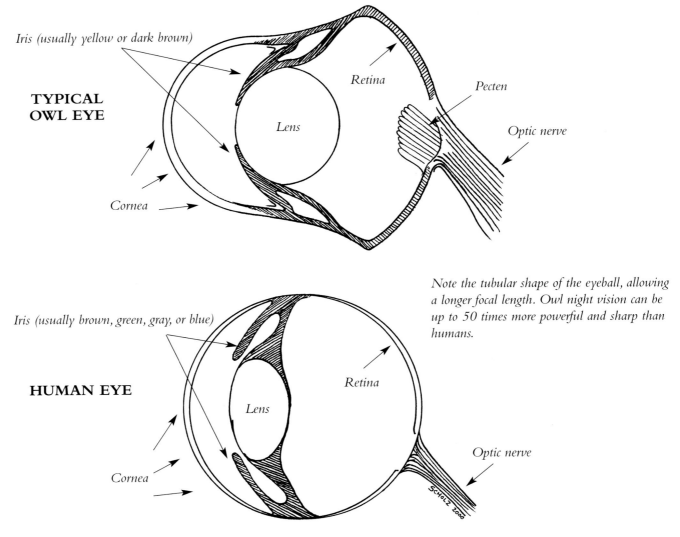

TYPICAL OWL EYE

Iris (usually yellow or dark brown)

Retina

Pecten

Optic nerve

Lens

Cornea

HUMAN EYE

Iris (usually brown, green, gray, or blue)

Retina

Lens

Optic nerve

Cornea

Note the tubular shape of the eyeball, allowing a longer focal length. Owl night vision can be up to 50 times more powerful and sharp than humans.

Birds and reptiles possess an organ called a pecten, which mammals do not. It is believed that this organ helps in the maintenance of eye structure—keeping it healthy, moist, and ensuring correct chemical balance.

eagles, and vultures, the presence of many cones (as well as unique cone modifications) has bestowed on them keen visual powers. With owls and other nocturnal creatures, the reverse is true. Their eyes have many more rods than cones, giving them the incredible ability to make the most of whatever ambient light is available.

To provide such powers of low-light vision, owl eyes must be very large and sensitive. If our eyes were in the same proportion to the size of our head as are the eyes of an owl, they would be the size of grapefruits. To accommodate these huge eyes, a few sacrifices must be made. Owls cannot move their eyes within their eye sockets; they are fixed and directed forward. To compensate, owls have developed extremely supple necks that allow them to turn their heads approximately 270 degrees. (This can be done so fast that it

was once thought that owls could spin their heads completely around. An old wives' tale says that if you walk around a perched owl enough times, its head will twist right off.)

Owls' forward-facing, humanlike eyes give them excellent binocular vision, a trait shared by diurnal raptors, herons, egrets, and many fish-catching seabirds. Although their vision encompasses only half the span of human vision, owls have extraordinary depth perception, which is essential as they make instant adjustments when closing in on a scurrying mouse or racing rabbit. Tests have revealed that the depth perception of owls is far more acute than that of any other bird. To enhance depth perception, owls often make a series of bobbing and jerking motions while focusing; this helps them triangulate the location of their prey.

This extreme close-up of the eye of an adult saw-whet owl reveals a transition not only in color but also in feather structure inherent to the facial disk makeup of this and other owl species. The dark colored feathering immediately surrounding the eye has perhaps evolved to reduce glare.

A black orb appears to float within a cauldron of molten yellow. The eye of this snowy owl is enveloped in the driftlike white feathering of its facial disk feathers. Snowy owls, both male and female, have absolutely no markings on their facial disks.

Utter perfection in form, flow, and function is revealed in this short-eared owl's facial disk, showing the subtle, intricate beauty of this species.

Intensity and conviction are evident in the watchful gaze of this great gray owl. Note the exact spacing of the concentric rings that radiate out from the glowing yellow eye.

This extreme close-up of a northern hawk owl shows the variation in the structure of the facial disk of this superbly adapted species. Northern hawk owls possess one of the most undeveloped facial disks of any owl species, rivaled only by the burrowing owl.

The complex interplay of the various feather groups and transition zones under the throat is revealed. Note the distinct black bib and the shift from beak to feathers. Also shown is the unobstructed field of vision below the eyes.

The facial disk of a barred owl seems to draw you in closer and closer, almost absorbing you into the structural delicacy of the plumage. Note the transition from the outer perimeter feathers of this beautiful owl.

As if in a state of constant surprise, this long-eared owl possesses the bulging yet wondrous eyes inherent to this species. This owl is not happy, as evidenced by the tightly laid back ear tufts.

Finely tuned and gracefully shaped parabolic reflectors are set off by the glistening dark eyes set deep within the facial disk of this beautiful barn owl.

The interplay of the wispy filoplumes of this barn owl helps direct and focus sound waves back to the unevenly placed ears located on the outer rims of the facial disk.

This is the look that strikes terror in the heart of any lemming or north woods mouse. Note the eye-to-beak geometry.

A profile of a great gray owl shows off the prominence and color of the beak and its relationship to the eyes.

This gray-phase eastern screech-owl illustrates the importance of understanding the "traffic jam" of feathering in front of the eyes and around the beak.

This three-quarter viewing angle reveals a red-phase screech-owl's nictitating membrane spanning the eye in a diagonal direction, keeping the eye clean and free of debris.

Note the prominence of the stiff rictal bristles as they fan out from in front of the eyes, extending quite far beyond the beak.

This head position of a gray-phase screech-owl illustrates how the throat feathers are compressed. When the bird emits a hoot, this area expands tremendously.

Being largely diurnal in its lifestyle and hunting tactics, this burrowing owl relies more on sight than on hearing, as evidenced by its undeveloped facial disk. Compare this shape to that of the highly nocturnal barn owl.

The nictitating membrane, otherwise known as the third eyelid, keeps the sensitive eyeball of this barred owl well lubricated and free of airborne dust.

Well-balanced proportion and mesmerizing feather flow are hallmarks of the short-eared owl's face.

In this close-up three-quarter view of the eye and facial disk of a short-eared owl, the black lines radiating from the dark ring surrounding the eye create a directional rhythm, offset by the whiter feathers surrounding the inner part of the eye.

The converging feather tracts create a surreal pattern, and the interplay of light and dark, sharp and soft, seems to hold the viewer in a hypnotic trance.

Note the variation in color and density of the feathers as they encircle the eye in this profile of a short-eared owl.

Such sensitive and precise ocular equipment needs to be well protected and maintained. Like all diurnal raptors, owls possess a nictitating membrane, or "third eyelid." This opaque lens slides across the front of the eye from the inner corner upward, lubricating and cleansing the outer surface of the cornea. The nictitating membrane is used in situations when the eyes might be injured or scratched, such as when an adult feeds enthusiastic chicks or subdues thrashing prey. Owls' outer eyelids close from the top down, the same as humans' but different from most other birds'. How could anyone not be charmed by a creature that winks?

HEARING

Even more important than eyesight to a hungry owl—especially the purely nocturnal hunters—is its miraculous sense of hearing. Structurally, all the elements of an owl's head—facial disk shape, slope, and feathering—work together to channel incoming sound waves into the ear openings. These openings, called external auditory meatuses, are located on both sides of the facial disk and are of different sizes; additionally, one is set higher than the other. Each opening has a flap of skin that can shift position and change the shape of the ear cavity to maximize sound collection. The feathers that surround the opening also help steer sound waves into the ear canal. The placement of the meatuses varies greatly among different owl species, as does hearing ability in general. Forest hunters, such as the great gray owl, spotted owl, barred owl, and boreal owl, have the most highly developed sense of hearing.

The ear tufts, which are a distinctive feature of eared owls' appearance, have nothing at all to do with hearing. The tufts are thought to play a role in courtship, camouflage, and display.

OWL HEAD TOPOGRAPHY

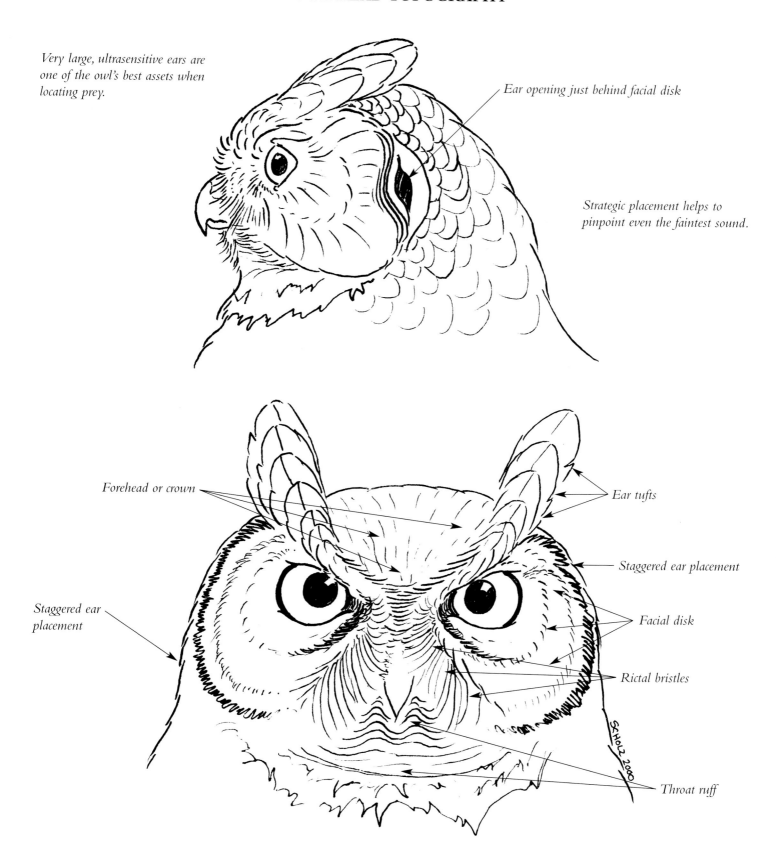

Very large, ultrasensitive ears are one of the owl's best assets when locating prey.

Ear opening just behind facial disk

Strategic placement helps to pinpoint even the faintest sound.

Forehead or crown

Ear tufts

Staggered ear placement

Staggered ear placement

Facial disk

Rictal bristles

Throat ruff

The matted density and intricate structure of the facial disk feathering of this barred owl combine to direct oncoming sound waves into the ear openings.

Like a small entry to a large cave, the ear opening, barely visible, belies a huge, cavernous ear chamber beneath.

The development and structure of the nostrils and cere region of the beak of this burrowing owl are clearly revealed.

The top of a barn owl's head reveals the patchwork of tight, patterned areas of vermiculation interspersed throughout the head and back regions.

Simply stated, if you are a mouse or other small rodent and see this coming at you, you're dead!

In Charlie Chaplinesque fashion, this barn owl waves its head from side to side to aid in pinpointing the location of a sound.

FRANK MCMAHON

WING DESIGN AND FEATHER STRUCTURE

As a boy of fifteen, I struck out on my own one winter day into the woods of northern Maine, hoping to prove my hunting prowess. I quickly became lost, hopelessly disoriented, and increasingly frightened. Then I heard the snap of a breaking limb behind me. I wheeled around, my heart pounding, and found myself staring into a pair of piercing, glowing eyes. I realized I was face-to-face with the biggest owl I had ever seen in my life. I'll never forget watching that great gray bird take flight, float down a ravine, and disappear into an embrace of green spruce boughs and hemlock branches. What astonished me most was that when this enormous creature took to the air, it was utterly silent. How on earth could a bird with a five-foot wingspan fly without making a sound?

I soon learned that an owl's flight feathers have a number of characteristics which enable the bird to fly silently. Overall, the wing feathers are soft and supple— if you ever have the opportunity to compare an owl's feathers with those of a red-tailed hawk, for example, you'll notice the difference in texture immediately. Also, an owl's wing-tip feathers, called primaries, have specially modified edges that muffle the air rushing over them. The primaries also have hairlike fringes that help stifle sound. Silent flight is important to an owl for two reasons: It allows the owl to surprise its prey, and it allows the owl to hear even a tiny squeak or the whisper of a mouse's footstep on the darkest of nights.

Opposite page: The barred owl's ear openings are situated toward the lower portion of the outer facial disk. Note the abrupt change in shape and structure between the facial disk feathers and the contour feathers of the overall head.

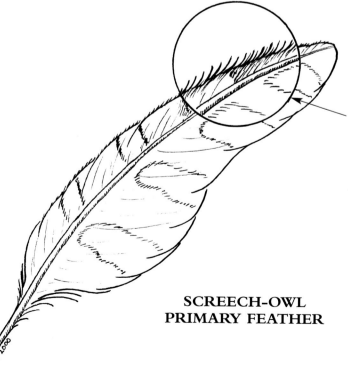

Nocturnal owls have the ability to fly noiselessly due to the unique feather design. The outside edges of flight feathers have downy edges that eliminate the "whooshing" noise of a stiff feather.

SCREECH-OWL PRIMARY FEATHER

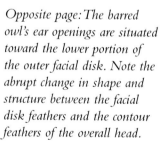

TYPICAL OWL FEATHER TOPOGRAPHY

Ear tufts

Eye

Head

Facial disks

Beak

Nape

Throat ruff

Patagial area or wrist

Scapulars

Upper coverts

Tertials (4)

Secondary coverts (14)

Leg

Foot

Under tail coverts

Talons

Secondaries (14)

Tail feathers (12)

Primaries (10)

Known as the "tiger of the air" the great horned owl shows off the splendid coloring and powerful build that make it the unchallenged master of the nighttime skies.

This great horned owl's attention has been diverted to something happening below. Body posture and shifting balance are subtle indicators of the bird's mood and intent. Notice the flow and dynamic position of the scapular feathers and the major flight feathers. Wonderful foot position is shown, as well as breast feathering.

ANATOMY OF A TYPICAL
OWL WING
(SAW-WHET OWL)

TOP VIEW

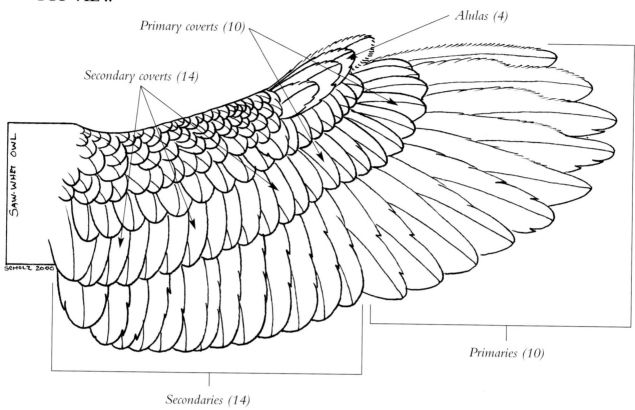

Primary coverts (10)

Secondary coverts (14)

Alulas (4)

SAW-WHET OWL

SCHOLZ 2000

Primaries (10)

Secondaries (14)

UNDERSIDE

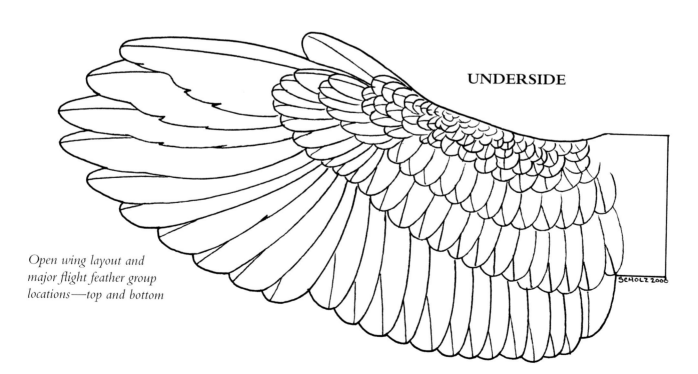

Open wing layout and major flight feather group locations—top and bottom

SCHOLZ 2000

Birds possess a fused backbone, so they have to rely on an extremely supple and long neck to access hard-to-reach areas while preening.

Body shape and dynamics can change drastically as the owl expands its feathers. This short-eared owl is beginning an action called rousing, which helps to realign and organize the feathers. It also traps fresh air against the body to assist in insulating the bird against the cold.

You can tell a lot about an owl's method of hunting and the time of day when it's most active by the shape and structure of the primary feathers, such as in this northern hawk owl's wing tip.

This long-eared owl's wing tip reveals a totally different structure from that of the northern hawk owl.

This is a flea's-eye view of the throat feathers of an adult barred owl.

The mobility and length of the barn owl are astonishing. Note the position of the legs and what happens when they join the body.

Perfection in shape, color, and purpose—the results of millions of years of fine-tuning—is what sets birds apart from all the other organisms on our planet. The wing feather of an adult barred owl is built for silent flight.

Notice how the upper chest feathers of this preening short-eared owl flow over the upper wing section and the loose belly feathers cascade downward toward the feet.

This preening short-eared owl shows the extreme mobility in the neck. Note the deflection that occurs in the upper chest feathers as they are realigned and cleaned.

The shape of an owl's wings has an effect on its flight characteristics. Typically, the rounder and shorter the wings, the slower, more buoyant, and more maneuverable the flier. The short, round wings of most owls have what is called a low aspect ratio. (Simply stated, aspect ratio is the ratio of wing chord to wingspan, as shown in the accompanying diagram.) The long, tapering wings of falcons and albatrosses, for example, which are more efficient for high-speed flight, have a high aspect ratio.

Even among owls, however, wing shape, and therefore aspect ratio, varies considerably. Owls that are more active during the day—northern hawk owls, snowy owls, and burrowing owls—have longer and narrower wings than do more nocturnal owls. These day-active

birds sacrifice a bit of stealth and maneuverability to gain a faster, more direct flight.

FEET AND TALONS

The future is not bright for a prey animal that finds itself in the path of an oncoming owl. An owl's feet are veritable aerial traps, with a number of features that help them grab and hang on to a prey item until it is dead. Under normal circumstances, when an owl flies, it draws its legs and feet up close to its belly, clenching its talons tightly. When it dives on prey, however, an owl brings its feet forward, fully extends its legs, and holds it talons wide open. On impact, the needle-sharp talons usually plunge deep into the prey. As the legs bend, thick tendons along the back of the legs snap the talons

HIGH ASPECT RATIO WING
(typical falcon; faster, less manueverable flight)

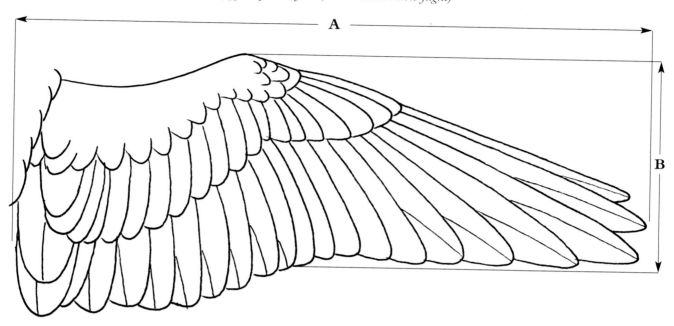

LOW ASPECT RATIO WING
(saw-whet owl; slower, more manueverable flight)

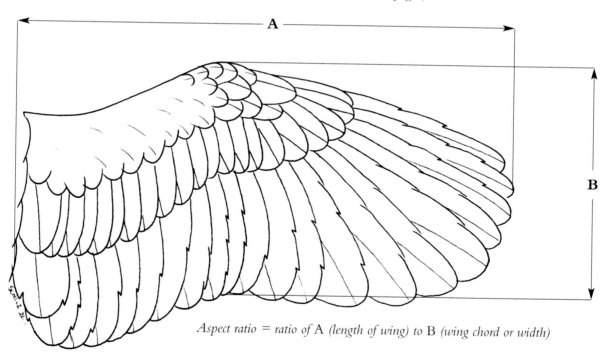

Aspect ratio = ratio of A *(length of wing) to* B *(wing chord or width)*

Aspect ratio is the term used to define the method of flight and its direct connection with the size and shape of the wing of a bird. A peregrine falcon, with long, narrow tapered wings, can fly extremely fast and is capable of blinding speeds in a vertical dive. To accomplish this, it has given up a degree of manueverability and cannot flap its wings as fast as a similarly sized owl. High aspect ratio wing design is aerodynamically more efficient, which is why most soaring birds have this configuration. Low aspect ratio wings enable a bird to navigate through even the densest of undergrowth while flying. Short, explosive bursts of speed and quick agile turns are hallmarks of a bird possessing this type of wing design. The wings of most owl species fall into this category.

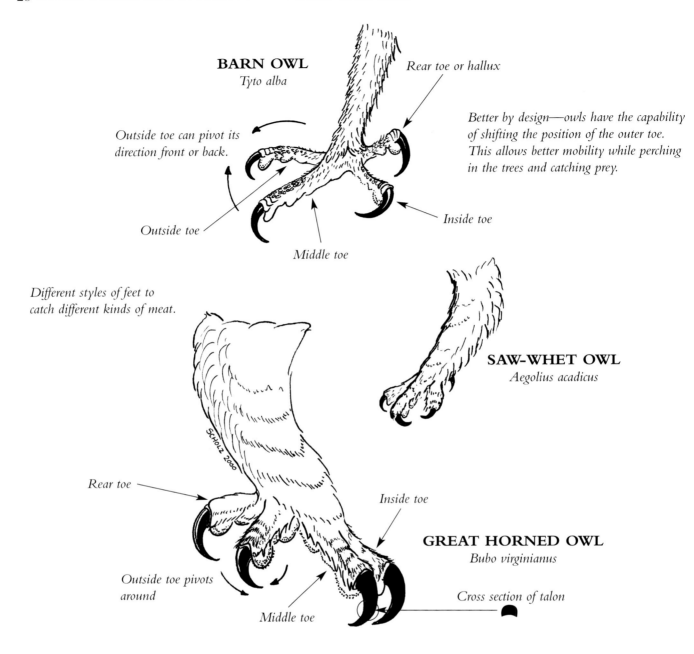

BARN OWL
Tyto alba

Rear toe or hallux

*Outside toe can pivot its
direction front or back.*

*Better by design—owls have the capability
of shifting the position of the outer toe.
This allows better mobility while perching
in the trees and catching prey.*

Outside toe

Inside toe

Middle toe

*Different styles of feet to
catch different kinds of meat.*

SAW-WHET OWL
Aegolius acadicus

Rear toe

Inside toe

GREAT HORNED OWL
Bubo virginianus

*Outside toe pivots
around*

Cross section of talon

Middle toe

shut. Scientists and bird banders who work with owls can give testament to the sharpness of an owl's talons and the amazing strength of its grip.

Owls possess a unique toe configuration shared by only one other raptor, the osprey. The owl's outer toe is reversible, giving the bird the ability to perch in either a tridactyl (with three toes forward and one toe backward, like most songbirds) or a zygodactyl (with two toes forward and two toes backward, like parrots and woodpeckers) formation. This flexibility allows owls to seize their prey in the most effective manner possible.

An owl's legs are protected from the exertions of captured prey and are kept warm in the winter by a covering of dense feathers which extends all the way to the feet. The exception in North America is the burrowing owl, which has bare legs.

BEAKS

Owls must overcome and kill their prey in order to survive. This is usually accomplished with the feet; attacking with the beak would put the owl's eyes in harm's way. Only very rarely does an owl attack or kill by biting. Most often, the strongly hooked and sharp beak is used to tear up already-dead prey that is too large to swallow whole.

An owl's beak is longer than it looks; often, only the tip is visible through the fluffy feathers on the face.

Extreme power and strength are hallmarks of the magnificent great horned owl, also known as the "tiger of the nighttime skies."

The foot of a great horned owl illustrates a zygodactyl toe configuration—two toes forward, two toes backward—permitting superior perching, climbing, and prey-grabbing abilities. Notice the extreme density of the feathering.

This barn owl's foot is quite a contrast to that of the great horned owl.

But it is every bit as lethal. The barn owl is a champion mouser.

Pay particular attention to the placement of the rear toe, or hallux, of this perched short-eared owl.

Ideally suited for life in a frigid environment, these well-protected feet of a snowy owl conceal long, powerful, rapier-like talons. Note the softness and density of the plumage as it gently cascades down and overlaps the toes. Snowy owls can completely cover their feet with their dense belly feathers to lock out the unforgiving north winds.

Note the size difference but similar design in the feet of a barred owl and a saw-whet owl.

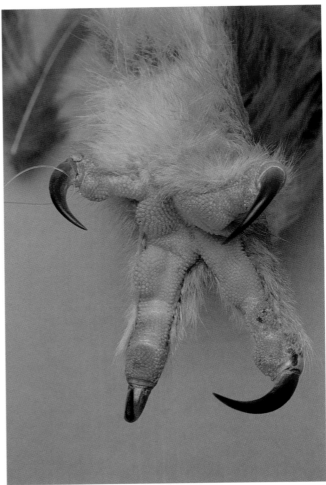

The right tool for the job is a formula for success, as the business end of a barred owl shows.

The deadly weaponry can be completely concealed by the soft, furlike covering of the foot.

Note the coloring and fleshlike quality of these toes of an eastern screech-owl.

The foot of a great gray owl, although not as large or powerful as that of its southern cousin the great horned owl, is every bit as deadly to prey.

A barred owl's foot shows the structure and density of the plumage from the upper leg to the tips of the toes. This offers a good defense against its prey, which can inflict horrible bites as it fights for its life. Notice the needlelike sharpness of the talons and the pebbly texture of the fleshy pads on the bottom of the foot.

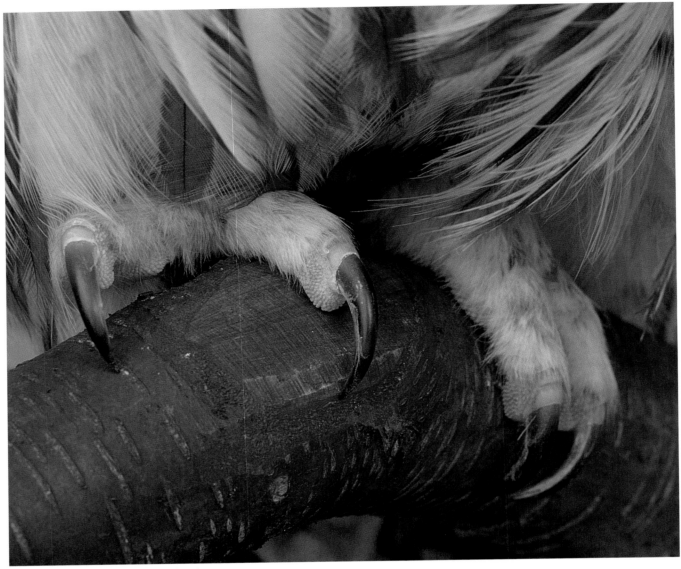

A close-up of the feet of a barred owl.

Unlike diurnal birds of prey, the owl's beak is positioned low on the face and is curved sharply downward. These adaptations keep the beak well clear of the owl's all-important field of vision. The owl's nostrils are located quite far forward toward the base of the bill. This region, called the cere, is not as supple and fleshy as is that of other raptors.

Tests indicate that most owls have a very poor sense of smell. It must be true: I've been around more than one great horned owl that absolutely reeked of skunk from a recent meal.

COLORATION

Even among the species that inhabit the tropics, there are no brightly colored owls. An owl's true beauty is in the soft, subtle browns of its plumage and in the infinitely complex series of stripes, spots, chevrons, bars, and streaks with which it is adorned. Unlike eagles, hawks, and falcons, an owl's age and sex cannot be determined by its coloration or by variations in its plumage. After an immature owl molts into its adult plumage, it retains that same color and feather pattern throughout its life.

The deep, dark, magical eyes of a northern spotted owl appear like two bottomless inkwells. Note the color and shape of the beak and the design of the nostrils.

Ever vigilant and eagerly anticipating their next meal, these baby great horned owls are already exhibiting traits that will put them at the apex of the food chain: big eyes, sharply hooked beaks, and razor-sharp talons.

Note the beautiful transition from spots to vertical barring on the chest and belly of this barred owl.

Screech-owls are difficult to see when they perch motionless against the rough bark of a tree—a miraculous job of camouflage. Typically, gray-phase screech-owls are more prevalent in the extreme northern forests, their color more closely replicating the bark of huge pine and spruce trees.

The facial disk of an adult saw-whet owl reveals a subtle transition of color and the interplay of white and brown.

Dappled sunlight filtering through the trees, combined with a dazzling array of green and brown textures and tones, provides the perfect forest backdrop for the spotted owl to seemingly vanish into its wooded domain.

The Species

EARED VS. NON-EARED

In undertaking the awesome task of assembling the information and visual material for this book, my intention was not to produce an authoritative ornithological textbook. As an artist who works in three dimensions, it is the visual charm and complex personalities of birds that I find most appealing. I discovered early on that I am drawn to birds' physical beauty and variety rather than to raw scientific data. Thus I took the liberty of organizing the species of North American owls based on their outward physical characteristics. Directing my decision were criteria such as the presence of ear tufts, similarity of plumage, and size.

EAR TUFTS

The two well-developed tracts of feathers located above the eyes in many species of owls are often referred to as ears. This misnomer has taken hold so deeply in the vernacular that two species have it as part of their name—the short-eared and long-eared owls. Even the mightiest owl of them all has its tufts referred to as horns—the great horned owl.

The purpose of these feathers is much more than mere decoration. They are an important part of the overall reason owls look the way they do: camouflage. Studies have shown that when an eared owl is at rest or not feeling threatened, it has the ability to relax these marker feathers, which then lie down and conform to the slope of the head. But the instant the owl feels a need to become "invisible," it draws itself up tall and thin. Sometimes, as in the case of a long-eared owl, the bird actually modifies the shape of its facial disk, making it vertical and thin, and fully erects those elongated groups of feathers to help the owl better blend with its wooded background. Over the years, countless eager bird-watchers have no doubt "glassed" right past an old broken branch sticking out of a tree, only to have it vanish after a second look.

EARED OWLS

WESTERN SCREECH-OWL
Ótus kénnicottii

EASTERN SCREECH-OWL
Ótus ásio

WHISKERED SCREECH-OWL
Ótus trichôpsis

GREAT HORNED OWL
Búbo virginiánus

SHORT-EARED OWL
Ásio flámmeus

LONG-EARED OWL
Ásio ótus

GREAT HORNED OWL
Búbo virginiánus
lighter plumage as found in desert areas

FLAMMULATED OWL
Ótus flamméolus

Eastern Screech-Owl
Otus asio

Otus asio, meaning "eared owl" or "horned owl," is the only small owl with feathered ear tufts that breeds in the eastern half of the continental United States. This feisty little hunter occurs in two distinct color phases—the red phase, which is actually a russet or sienna color, and the gray phase, which can vary from slate gray to dark brownish gray. (The other two screech-owl species, the western screech-owl and the whiskered screech-owl, are not covered because they are virtually identical in physical appearance to the gray-phase eastern screech-owl.)

Referring to this magical little bird as a screech-owl is like calling Luciano Pavarotti a cackling human. If you've ever had the opportunity to hear its mellow, plaintive whinnying, followed by a series of downward-spiraling tremulous whistles, you would no doubt come to the same conclusion. However, in many backwoods regions of rural America, the screech-owl was looked on as a bad omen whose mournful song could impart death or misfortune to all within earshot. Rituals were routinely practiced to ward off the inevitable dire consequences.

The screech-owl is a fairly common breeding bird throughout the East and seems quite happy in a variety of habitats, from city parks to dense hemlock and spruce thickets, woodlots, and suburban backyards. These nonmigratory owls have learned to exploit a variety of food items. They hunt small mammals, earthworms, snakes, moths, beetles, frogs, and fish. Even agile songbirds think twice before relaxing around a pair of hungry screech-owls.

No one knows this better than my friend and world-renowned artist Guy Coheleach, who shared with me a story of screech-owls in his backyard. Years ago when he and his family lived on Long Island, Guy recalls knowing the birds so well that he could determine whether or not the owls had eaten that day based on their attitude and facial expressions. He said, "The ones who had eaten had a look of contentment as they sat fluffed and satiated on the overhanging branches in my backyard. In sharp contrast were the burning, intense focus and deliberate aggressive actions of the hungry predators who had not fed that day. You could see it in their eyes."

The big, bright eyes of a screech-owl are well suited for its strictly nocturnal lifestyle. These large eyes are deeply seated in two well-developed facial disks, which direct sound back to the hypersensitive ears. The lovely little face is framed by two dark brown arcs separating the front half of the face from the back of the head. The back scapular feathers are edged in two bright rows of white feathers, each singularly tipped in dark brown. The major flight feathers are subtly barred in darker brown, and the primaries are edged in white bars.

SPECIES PROFILE

1. The only small eared owl breeding east of the Mississippi River.
2. Occurs in two distinct color phases: red and gray.
3. Call is a plaintive, wailing whistle of descending notes.
4. An opportunistic feeder. Takes a wide range of prey, sometimes tackling animals bigger than itself.
5. A nonmigratory, year-round resident in its breeding range.
6. Strictly nocturnal in its habits; it sits quietly during the daylight hours, standing tall and thin next to a tree trunk with ear tufts erect.
7. Very aggressive in nest defense and has been known to attack humans who come too close.
8. Nests in hollowed-out tree cavities or old woodpecker holes. Readily accepts man-made nest boxes.
9. Average length 7 to 9½ inches.
10. Surprisingly swift and agile flier despite its short-tailed, rather nonaerodynamic shape and design.

Eastern Screech-Owl
Otus asio

3¾"

3"

Eye
14mm yellow

8½"–10"

8"

3¼"

2¾"

1¾"

SCHOLZ 2000

As this owl turns its head to the side, note the beauty and order of the scapular feathers as they ascend to the beak. In this pose, they eventually fold into the fluffy pineconelike throat feathers located under the lower mandible.

A sleepy gray-phase screech-owl.

The owl begins to wake up; note the position of the ear tufts in relation to the eyes. Also shown is the dark brown perimeter of the facial disks.

Note the development and prominence of the rictal bristles as they fan outward from the inside corner of the eye of this red-phase screech-owl.

Is it tree bark or feathers? It's tough to tell as you look at the back of the head of a gray-phase screech-owl.

This close-up of the eye and beak region of an adult gray-phase screech-owl shows the subtle color blending that occurs around the beak. Also note the compressed pineconelike feathering under the beak.

Opposite page: Gorgeous coloration and variety of markings in the wing and face of a red-phase screech-owl.

The eyelids appear to protrude away from the surface of the eyeball itself.

An endearing, humanlike quality of all owls is that when they blink, their eyelids close from the top downward, giving rise to the notion of the wise, all-knowing owl.

An extremely complex structure makes up the facial disk filoplumes surrounding the eyes of this gray-phase screech-owl. See how they overlap the much darker arcs that frame the face.

The form and flow of the white eyebrows are shown as these facial feathers trail downward around the eye, gradually turning into the triangular "mustache" enveloping the beak.

A curious little red-phase screech-owl looks upward, wondering, "What's with all the lights and cameras?"

This back head view of a red-phase screech-owl reveals the placement and number of feathered ear tufts. If you looked quickly, you might think that you are looking at the back of a cat's head.

Screech-owls, like most owls, swallow their prey whole, so they need to be able to open their mouths quite wide. This gray-phase screech-owl reveals how much of the mouth lies hidden under the rictal bristles. Note the pink color of the mouth lining.

This close-up of a gray-phase screech-owl details the complex coloring and patterning of the iris.

Observe the dynamic flow of chest, breast, and belly feather tracts set against the solid white markings of the leading edge of the wing.

This view of a gray-phase screech-owl illustrates the relationship of the tertial, secondary, and primary feathers that make up the propulsion part of the wing.

Profile of an adult red-phase screech-owl.

The beautiful scapular feathers seem to cascade gently off the upper wrist of the owl. Note the dark brown centers and blended tips.

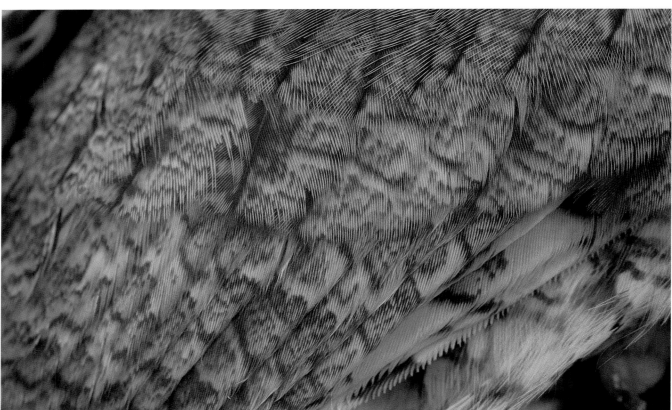

Note the sawtooth design of the edges of the flight feathers, enabling silent, stealthy flight.

Notice the pleasing flow between feather groups of this red-phase screech-owl.

This gray-phase screech-owl has much more complex, cryptic patterning in its contour feathers than the red-phase bird.

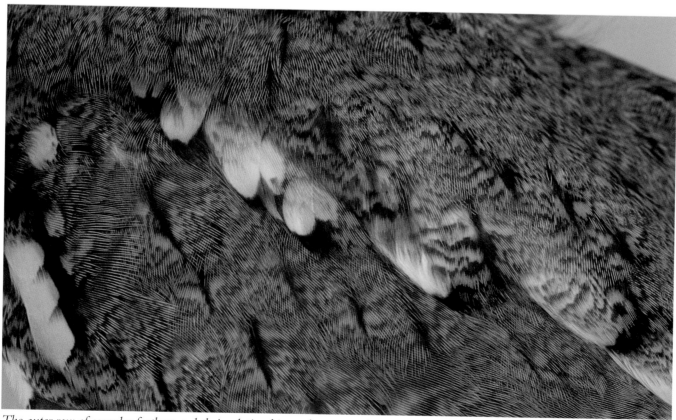

The outer row of scapular feathers and their relationship to the upper wing region.

The plumage of this gray-phase screech-owl resembles the thick, dense fur of a Canadian lynx.

Overall view of the upper tail surface and upper tail coverts of a red-phase screech-owl. Notice the subtle barring of the feathers.

An avalanche of markings and textures flows gracefully down and around the toes.

Lower back region of a red-phase screech-owl. Notice the size and direction of the dark brown markings.

A macroview of the preceding photograph reveals the feather structure to be almost hairlike.

Note the deflection in the transition zone feathers of this red-phase screech-owl.

Silent flight is made possible by feathers such as these.

Subtlety and softness define the underside of the wing of a red-phase screech-owl.

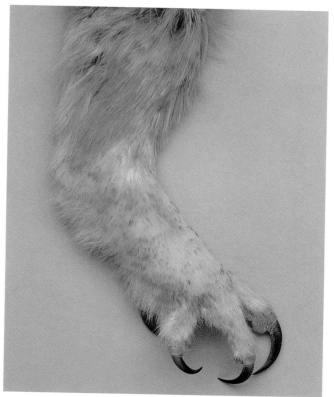

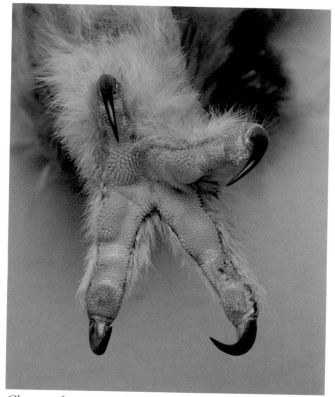

The business end of a red-phase screech-owl.

Chances of escape are minimized by such deadly weaponry.

Note the variation in shape and size of these primary feathers of a red-phase screech-owl.

Close-up of the feet and toes of a gray-phase screech-owl.

This series of pictures is a study in proportion and pose. The extremely well-defined and well-developed tertial feathers are clearly visible, as are the strongly arced primary feathers. This sequence also reveals the many attitudes and moods that can be transmitted by subtle nuances in head position and tilt.

Flammulated Owl
Otus flammeolus

This small, secretive owl of the extreme western United States and Mexico is the smallest eared owl on the continent. Distinguishable from its other small cousins by its dark, impassionate eyes, this owl was not classified until about 1853 by German naturalist Johann Kaup. In fact, a nest site was not described until twenty-two years later, in 1875. This owl is structured similar to the diminutive elf owl and seems to be the North American version of the scops owl found throughout the European continent.

Probably due to its small size and incredibly cryptic patterning, the flammulated owl is very hard to see as it perches motionless next to the rough trunk of a high-country pine tree. Compared with the other owl species, this small woodland nymph has gone largely unstudied.

Being one of the more highly migratory owls, flammulateds range from Washington State south to Mexico and Guatemala. Rare wanderers have even been seen as far east as Florida.

Just like its close relative the screech-owl, the flammulated owl is nocturnal in its habits and can best be located by its call, although its ventriloquistic abilities have led many an owl prowler astray. Flammulated owls have evolved a very low, deep call that is audible for quite a distance, probably to compensate for this tiny owl's rather large territory.

Flammulated owls are cavity nesters and prefer to hunt and forage among the deep thickets bordering broken open country. They have been reported to readily accept nest boxes put out for kestrels. Relatively small clutches of three to four eggs are laid. Small clutch sizes are typically a reflection of a more stable lifestyle, one that is not greatly affected by the unpredictable fluctuations in prey availability felt by other, predominantly larger, northern species.

Flying in the darkest of night, this agile predator feeds on moths, many nocturnal insects, and even spiders. Catching its prey with its beak, it flits from tree to tree with rapid wing beats. If discovered roosting during the daylight hours, it raises its ear tufts to a vertical position and draws itself up to mimic a tree branch, rendering itself virtually invisible.

The russet-colored streaks that predominate the back area give this owl its name (flammulated means flame-colored), and its intricate vermiculated plumage pattern is thought to be the most complex of any North American owl species. When viewed from the front, the chest and belly are heavily streaked with dark brown vertical markings. There are both reddish and gray morphs. Birds that inhabit the northern reaches of its range tend to be the gray form, and reddish morphs predominate down south.

Flammulated owls have relatively long legs for their size and possess long, thin toes tipped with needlelike hooked talons. The thin little beak is silvery gray in color, graduating to buff or yellow at the tip.

SPECIES PROFILE

1. Smallest of the North American eared owls.
2. Only small North American owl with dark brown eyes.
3. Highly migratory, with a range from Washington State to southern Mexico.
4. Occurs in two distinct color phases: gray and red.
5. Feeds on moths, insects, and spiders.
6. Nests in hollowed-out cavities and averages fairly small clutch sizes—usually three to four eggs.
7. Its voice is a low-pitched, resonant *hoot,* repeated every few seconds.
8. Legs are feathered down to the upper parts of the scaled toes.
9. Prefers the rugged high country throughout the Rocky Mountains and above 4,000 feet.
10. Has an extremely fine and intricate plumage pattern that renders it invisible against the bark of big pine and spruce trees.

Eye
12mm black

3"
Body width at wrist area

Flammulated Owl
Otus flammeolus

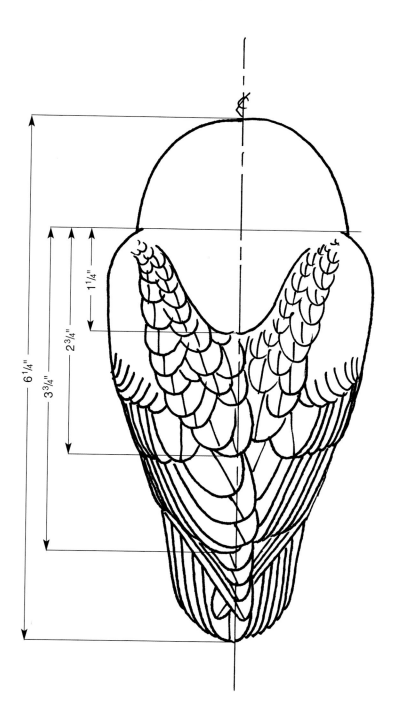

2¹/₄"

6¹/₄"

3³/₄"

2³/₄"

1¹/₄"

SCHOLZ 2000

A full frontal view shows feather flow and textural variety of the chest and belly feathers. Notice the relatively small facial disks and proportionately large eyes.

FRANK MCMAHON

These birds can seemingly melt into the forest, thanks to their cryptic patterning and coloration.

FRANK MCMAHON

Large light-gathering eyes enable this little owl to forage with ease, even on the blackest of nights.

FRANK MCMAHON

This little owl was photographed at a raptor rehabilitation center. Note the intensity in the eyes and the feather overlap in the upper chest region onto the wing.

FRANK MCMAHON

Note the direction and position of the outer edge of the scapular feather group.

FRANK MCMAHON

The cryptic patterning and coloration of this tiny hunter are evident in this full back view.

FRANK MCMAHON

This view of the upper surface of the fully extended wing shows the depth of the wing chord, extending fully below the upper tail coverts.

FRANK MCMAHON

The full underside of the opened wing of an adult flammulated owl.

Note the positioning of the alulae, primary coverts, and primary feathers and how they all relate to one another. The bright white spots on the leading edges of the primaries create an interesting contrast to the otherwise dark gray tones of the wing surface.

FRANK MCMAHON

The outer edges of the scapular feathers seem to converge, forming a distinct V above the upper tail coverts.

FRANK MCMAHON

Note the pebblelike texture of the skin covering the fleshy toe pads.

If looks could kill! This miniature dynamo must be getting tired of having its picture taken.

The breast and belly feathers flow around the leg, creating a nice contrast to the shiny black eye.

FRANK MCMAHON

FRANK MCMAHON

The upper tail coverts and the top of a badly worn tail.

FRANK MCMAHON

Looking like a piece of shaggy bark, this flammulated owl clings to the side of its flight enclosure.

Opposite page: Appearing almost alien, the face shows the beak-to-eye symmetry. Note the soft white brows and how they flow around the beak. FRANK MCMAHON

Long-eared Owl
Asio otus

Shy and secretive, this nocturnal denizen of the deep woods derives its name from the well-developed ear tufts set close together above its fiery, yellow-orange eyes. This crow-sized, slender owl is colored in beautiful earth tones and reddish sienna. It closely resembles the great horned owl in plumage but lacks the tight horizontal barring throughout the flank, belly, and chest regions, instead possessing a series of prominent vertical marks.

Long-eareds are a highly migratory species and, in contrast to their retiring nature during the summer months, can sometimes be viewed in great numbers perched amid the skeletonlike branches of deciduous trees during winter migration. In North America, two distinct races are found. The more common and wide-ranging tends to be darker and slightly larger than the southwestern race.

The long-eared owl is renowned for its amazing vocabulary. Its initial low baritone hoots can be heard for up to half a mile. Loud clicking, clacking, barking, and yipping have also been documented, especially during breeding season.

Like great horned owls, long-eareds prefer to nest out in the open, often taking advantage of old squirrels' nests or abandoned crows' nests, but they occasionally nest in a large tree cavity when nothing else is available. If a nest site is discovered, long-eared owls resort to a wide variety of tactics to deter a potential predator, ranging from aggressive aerial attacks to a killdeerlike broken wing display. They can also inflate themselves to double in size and hiss and clack threateningly.

Chipmunks, wood mice, and a large variety of other small animals make up the long-eared's diet. The owls hunt during the deepest hours of night, weaving silently through the tangle of forest growth in pursuit of their next meal.

The long-eared owl is known for its wide range of facial shapes, from perfectly circular to an apple shape with tall, erect ear tufts, giving the appearance of a broken piece of branch. The eyes can reveal the true mood of the bird. They may be set back in the facial disks or, in times of excitement, may seem to be almost popping out of the head. The ear openings in the skull run the whole length and are slightly offset from each other.

When perched, the long primary flight feathers almost reach the end of the tail, adding to this owl's streamlined, elongated form. The tail has six to seven dark brown bars.

To locate this elusive owl, concentrate your search on lower branches that are whitewashed from droppings. Long-eareds are birds of habit and often return to the same perch night after night.

SPECIES PROFILE

1. A medium-sized, slender owl with long, pronounced ear tufts set close together.
2. Nocturnal in its hunting forays.
3. Long wings provide exceptional maneuverability in flight.
4. Often seen perched in groups along migratory routes.
5. Feeds on assorted small rodents, small birds, and, occasionally, bugs.
6. Has a wide range of vocalizations, especially during the breeding and courtship season.
7. Inhabits the northern and northwestern regions of the United States and Canada.
8. Has bright yellow-orange eyes that are set deep in a russet-orange facial disk.
9. Overall cryptic feather pattern and color closely resemble those of a great horned owl.
10. Female long-eared owls are slightly bigger than males.

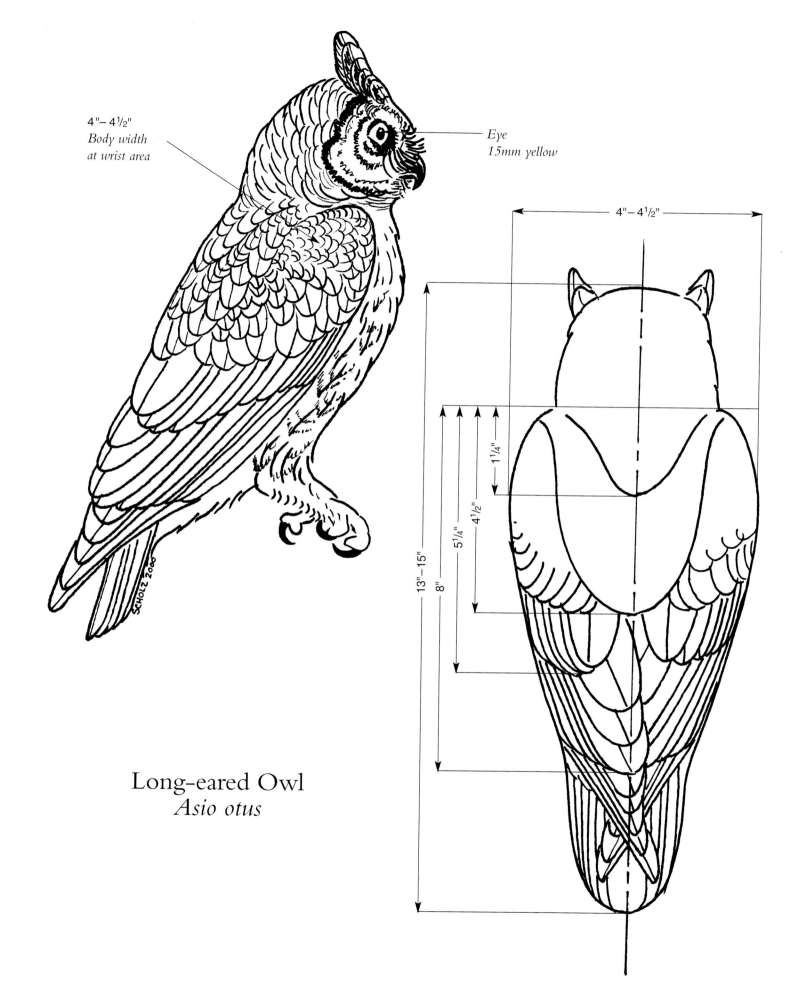

4"– 4½"
*Body width
at wrist area*

*Eye
15mm yellow*

SCHOLZ 2000

Long-eared Owl
Asio otus

4"– 4½"

1¼"

4½"

5¼"

8"

13"– 15"

A look of surprise is one of the many expressions of a long-eared owl.

A beautiful head profile shows the head shape geometry and the proportional distance between the eyes, ear tufts, and beak. Note the length of the rictal bristles.

The facial disk detail, eye position, and feather structure combine to give the owl its distinct appearance.

The forehead and top of the head have white spots and cryptic patterning.

Notice how the white brow feathers intermingle with the dark stripe that radiates upward from the top of the eye. The rictal bristles seem to explode outward from the inside circumference of the eye.

Suppleness in the neck region allows this owl an unrestricted range of vision, despite having eyes that are set in immovable sockets.

Another look at these soft, velvety feathers.

Full view of the back of the head.

Observe the beauty and complexity of these upper chest and belly feathers.

As the owl turns its head, very little deflection occurs in the lower feather areas.

The outer edges of the tertial and secondary feathers.

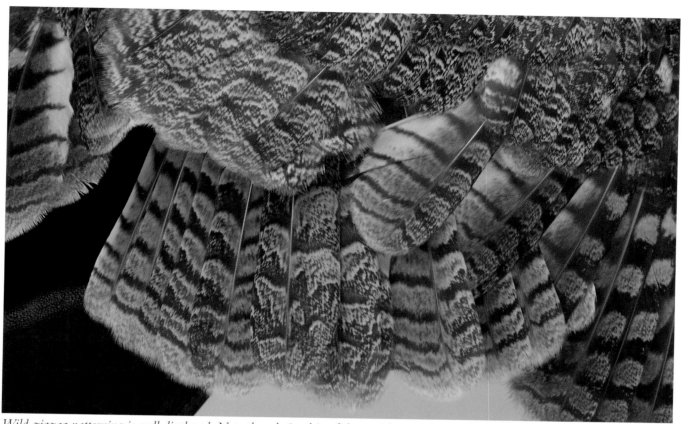

Wild zigzag patterning is well displayed. Note the relationship of the tertials, secondaries, and top surface of the tail.

Positioning of the back feathers and their relation to one another.

Notice the texture and design of the primary feathers, as well as the rippling waves.

Dynamic view of the upper region of the primary feathers. Note the transitions of color.

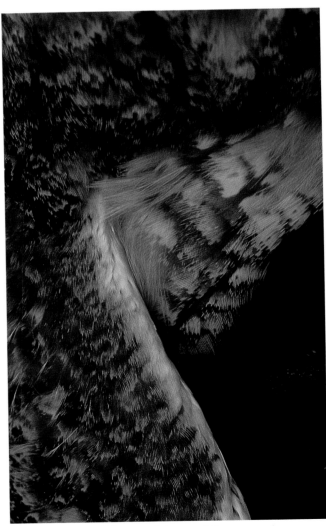

Transition zone of the patagial area of the upper wing.

Note the subtle vermiculations among the white bands of the primary feathers.

Opposite page: This owl is ready for action.

Short-eared Owl
Asio flammeus

This ground-nesting beauty has one of the largest worldwide distributions of any owl species, being found on every continent except Australia. The lifestyle of this crow-sized marsh owl, as it is sometimes called, is in sharp contrast to that of its more owl-like cousins. For starters, it hunts at all hours of the day but seems to be most active at dawn and dusk. Its method of hunting closely follows the ground-hunting style of the marsh hawk, rather than the camouflaged, sit-and-ambush style of other owls.

The short-eared owl has a raccoonlike appearance due to the distinctive dark patches surrounding its straw yellow eyes. Its fawn-colored belly is delicately patterned with vertical stripes that get thinner and longer as they cascade down the body toward the legs. It may be interesting to note that its scientific name, *Asio flammeus,* essentially means "flame-colored owl," a name bestowed upon it around 1763 by Danish naturalist Erik Pontoppidan. This seems odd, as the soft cryptic tan and brown coloration of this bird is far from exotic.

Even though the word "eared" appears in its name, these small tufts of feathers can hardly be seen. The tail and major flight feathers are heavily barred, and the top of the wings and back region up over the top of the head are covered in dark brown polka dots.

When sitting motionless on the ground among the high grass and reeds of its preferred habitat, the short-eared owl can be invisible—that is, until hunger or parental duties force it to take to the air, where it suddenly pops up from nowhere and begins scanning the meadows. Its flight is buoyed by long wings and busy, erratic wing beats.

Mice and other small mammals make up the bulk of its diet, but short-eared owls are opportunistic feeders and are not averse to eating insects or songbirds. They have long legs and long, slender toes tipped with needle-sharp talons.

In the field, these owls have the unique habit of sounding an alarm by clapping their wings sharply together under the belly area. The sound resembles a flag flapping in a strong wind and is audible for a surprising distance. Lifestyle and this odd behavior have all but erased the need for the broken-up hairlike fringes found on the leading edges of most other owls' flight feathers.

Short-eared owls need a lot of clear, open space to live—a requirement that is in direct competition with the needs of humans. Unfortunately, this lovely owl appears to be losing ground. There are fewer and fewer reports of short-eared owls nesting in areas where they were once common, such as the New Jersey coastline.

SPECIES PROFILE

1. A 13- to 17-inch mottled brown owl.
2. Nests on the ground or slight mound of earth centrally located in a marsh or field.
3. Feeds primarily on small rodents, but songbirds and large insects are frequently caught and eaten.
4. Long, well-developed wings almost completely cover the tail when folded.
5. Long-legged with fairly long, slender toes tipped with needle-sharp talons.
6. Bright yellow eyes seem small in relation to head size and are framed by dark rings, giving it a raccoonlike look.
7. Not very vocal, but seems more so during breeding and courtship season.
8. Tiny ear tufts are barely visible; when erect, they are located very close together above the eyes.
9. Uses a killdeerlike method of feigning injury to lure a potential predator away from the nest.
10. When viewed from the front, the belly and flanks appear heavily barred with vertical brown streaks.

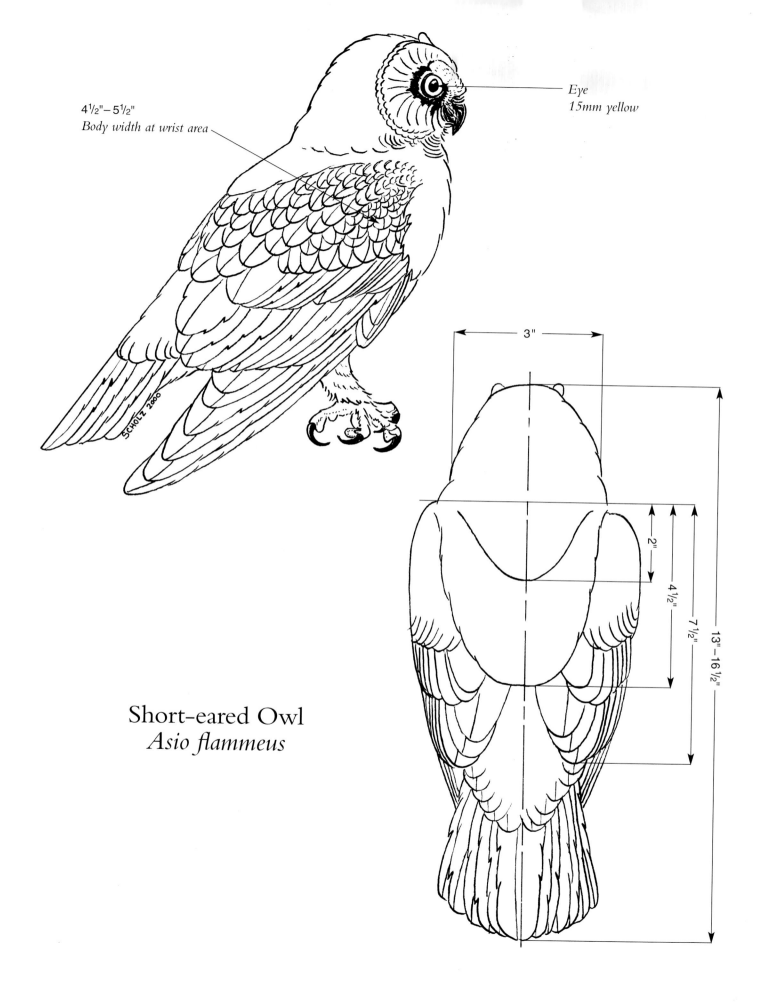

4¹⁄₂"– 5¹⁄₂"
Body width at wrist area

Eye
15mm yellow

3"

2"

4¹⁄₂"

7¹⁄₂"

13"– 16¹⁄₂"

SCHOLZ 2000

Short–eared Owl
Asio flammeus

This straight-on view reveals the proportionately small eyes in relation to the head. The top of the beak is on the same horizontal plane as the bottom of the eyes.

Note the soft, furlike quality of the upper chest feathers as they flow outward from the facial disk.

The feathering on the back of the head is so soft that it almost appears out of focus.

Note the pronounced bristle area in front of the eyes, as well as the shape and slope of the beak.

Head position is altered as the owl stretches to get a better look at something.

Another view of the same position.

The outer border of the facial disk is made up of highly dense, tiny spotted feathers.

This pose reveals a portion of the long left leg and the beautiful feather flow up the belly and into the chest.

Observe the intricacies of the feather structure throughout the facial disks, particularly the pattern of the small black feathers that radiate outward from the inside of the eye.

The extreme neck mobility of owls is legendary, as evidenced in this profile of a preening owl.

Back view of the head shows off the intricate feather flow.

The delicate white feathering under the beak gradually transforms into soft brown.

This is the upper chest region just below the facial disk.

Notice the fleshy pads under the toes—heavily dimpled and flesh-colored.

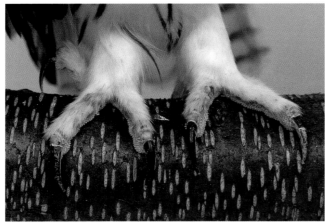

Long, supple toes are an asset when grabbing mice. Notice the dramatic position of the rear toe of the owl's right foot.

The whole wing is exposed.

This side view of the feet shows some flank feather overlap and provides a good look at the talons.

The upper right wing has a subtle blending of colors.

Rear view of the head of a preening owl. Head shape varies considerably as the bird contorts itself while grooming.

As the owl looks downward, feather deflection and fullness occur on top of the head.

Luxuriant feathering of the upper nape and neck.

This bird is stretching and beginning to rouse its feathers.

While preening its back, the owl's face gets lost in a wave of feathers.

Profile of the body and head. Note the relationship of the wing, foot, and head.

Spotting something on the ground, the owl shifts its weight over the right foot. Check out the dramatic positioning of the toes.

Upward stretching and extreme neck mobility allow the owl to preen its upper chest and neck regions.

Another preening owl.

A short-eared owl fluffing up against the cold. The owl's right wing primary feathers are dropped under the tail.

As the owl begins to rouse or shake out its feathers, the long, airy belly feathers seem to balloon out past the shorter, denser chest feathers.

Note the extreme elevation of the head, the separation of feathers just below the beak, and the expressive look in the eye.

This photo makes me laugh. It looks as though an explosion has occurred inside the owl.

Elevated nape feathers illustrate the extreme control the owl has over every single feather.

Balance is critical as this owl prepares to scratch an itch.

Marvel at the subtle shifting of feathers and wild contortions as the owl goes through a series of preening exercises.

All the preening is done, and the owl lets us know that everything is okay.

Note the appearance of the foot. A variety of head positions illustrates the amazing flexibility of the neck vertebrae.

Great Horned Owl
Bubo virginianus

Despite its imposing size and powerful frame, the most noticeable feature of a great horned owl is its glowing yellow eyes. Everything about the great horned owl radiates power. From its large size to its compact, powerful toes tipped with rapierlike talons, it is the very embodiment of a no-nonsense hunter.

This New World counterpart of the Eurasian eagle owl was not recognized as a separate species until around 1788, when the noted German-born naturalist Johann Gmelin's observations and descriptions of the great horned owl were published. Due to its highly adaptable nature and ability to nest in a variety of locations (from an abandoned red-tailed hawk's nest in the highest branches to the tall grass of an abandoned orchard), the great horned owl has become one of the most widespread of all North American owl species, resulting in descriptions of up to nineteen subspecies.

Its cryptic coloring ranges from dark slate gray in northeastern New England and Canada to an almost white fawnlike color in the northernmost reaches of the subarctic tundra and taiga. Its choice of prey items can be as variable as its color and range. Great horned owls are not fussy eaters and will consume anything they can kill, from small bugs to foxes, porcupines, and even skunks.

There are myriad bars and vermiculations throughout the body. Subtle washes of sienna and burnt umber accent and amplify the soft back and belly regions. An extremely soft, white throat bib sets the foundation for the eyes and the burnt sienna facial disks contained within parentheses of dark brown. The large, dark ears comprise up to seven feathers, and their position can reflect the mood of the owl. A word of caution: If the ear tufts are laid back tightly on the head and the beak is snapping and the owl is hissing, keep your distance.

SPECIES PROFILE

1. Large 18- to 25-inch owl with large yellow eyes.
2. Ear tufts are widely spaced and appear as large, dark horns.
3. Dark horizontal barring dominates the chest, breast, and belly.
4. Large, stout feet appear more furred than feathered and are tipped with large brownish black talons.
5. When roosting during the daylight hours, this large owl stands tall and perches near the trunk of a tree with its ear tufts standing straight up.
6. Its voice is a deep resonant series of hoots—*hoo, hoo-hoo-hoo, hoooo, hooooo.*
7. A nonmigrating, highly territorial owl that defends its nest and territory with ferocity.
8. Its wide range includes large city parks and open spaces, swamps, deserts, and forests up to extreme northern Canada.
9. Females can be up to 25 percent larger than males, but there is no discernible difference in color or plumage.
10. A highly nocturnal, extremely powerful predator.

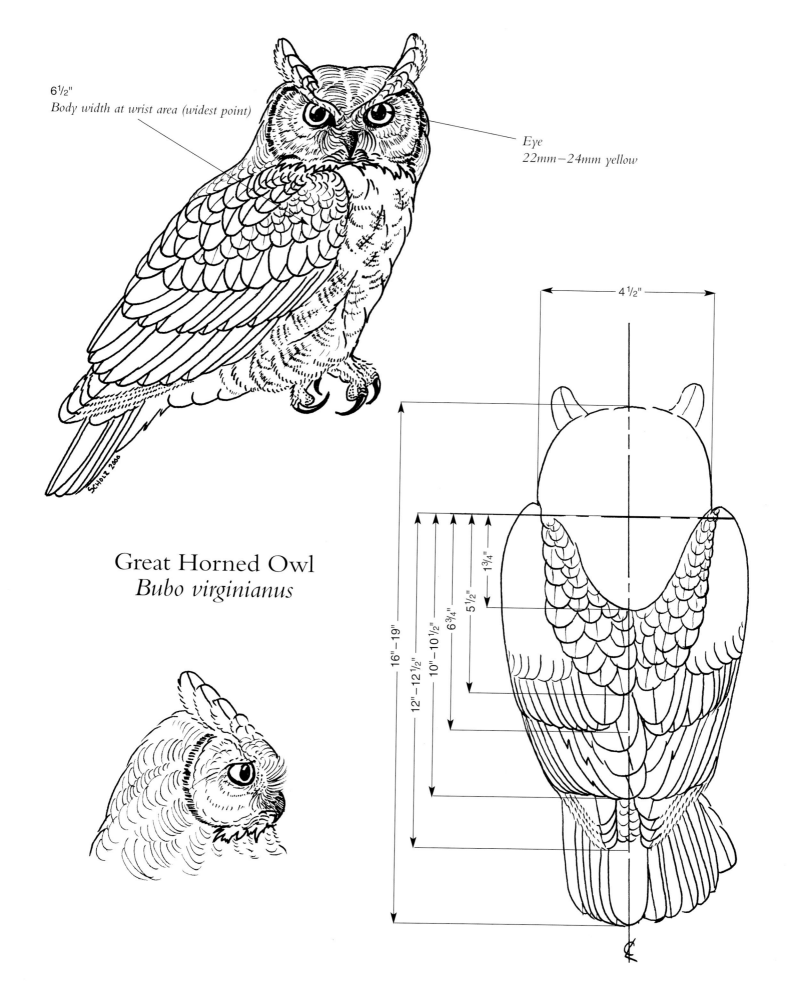

6½"
Body width at wrist area (widest point)

Eye
22mm−24mm yellow

Great Horned Owl
Bubo virginianus

4½"

16"−19"
12"−12½"
10"−10½"
6¾"
5½"
1¾"

Note the depth and intensity of the eye, as well as the eye-to-beak proportion.

Erect ear tufts angled above the eyes form opposing exclamation marks.

Partially closed eye shows both the coloration and the angle of the upper eyelid. Also note the nictitating membrane, or "third eyelid."

Full head profile illustrates the position of the dark facial disk frame and the angle of eye placement. Also, good eye-to-beak proportion is evident.

The face of an angry owl. Although only the extreme front part of the beak is visible past the facial fluff, when the owl opens its mouth, you get a sense of how far back the corners of the mouth are.

This owl seems to declare, "Come any closer and I'll bite off your nose!"

In this head profile looking down, pay close attention to the dark rictal bristles and where they radiate out from the eye.

Note the breakup and dynamic flow of the white bib or throat patch as the head turns to the right.

It is a real challenge to make visual sense of the mass of feathers that occurs at the lower corners of the head where it joins the body.

The throat patch has a soft, furlike quality—a beautiful collage of soft white and various browns.

FRANK MCMAHON

FRANK MCMAHON

Observe the flow and variation of feathers on the back of the head.

This action is called rousing. It helps realign the feathers and traps fresh warm air close to the body surface.

The feathering on the top of the head and forehead appears darker, with less distinct barring. Note the transition zones of white eyebrow feathers up onto the head.

Opposite page: Note the beautiful upper chest feather flow and the distinct dark brown spots below the white throat patch. Wind direction can be established by which way the ear tufts are blowing. FRANK MCMAHON

FRANK MCMAHON

A nice three-quarter front view.

FRANK MCMAHON

A vertical streak of pure white feathering seems to divide the chest into two parts. Note the spacing, rhythm, and shape of the horizontal barring throughout the flanks, chest, belly, and side of the head.

The amazingly soft nature of the chin and throat feathers is illustrated. Note the wavelike quality of the upper throat feathers and how they "pinecone" outward.

The infinite variety of brown tones and patterns can be a challenge.

Back view of an extreme head turn shows the dynamic feather flow in this area during a shift in feather placement.

FRANK MCMAHON

An alert and well-proportioned attitude is illustrated. Foot position can vary widely, depending on the type of perching situation.

FRANK MCMAHON

Look what happens to the white throat patch. It shifts its position in direct relationship to the location of the head.

Overlapping of the upper wrist area of the wing by the breast feathers.

Good balance and position are evident in this photo. The major flight feathers are hanging under the tail, an interesting and dynamic wing position that shows off the upper surface of the tail in a sitting position.

Rousing just prior to settling in.

The two forward-facing toes softly emerge from the lower belly feathers, creating a solid, balanced stance.

The slightly upward head tilt denotes a bit of curiosity.

FRANK MCMAHON

FRANK MCMAHON

The outer tail feathers are totally white with brown barring. Note the increasing waviness of the bars toward the end of the feather.

FRANK MCMAHON

In this back view of the top of the tail, you can barely see the difference between the top part of the right wing and the upper surface of the tail.

A great horned owl caught in motion, illustrating great leg, body, and wing position. This is a good animation reference.

The owl stands with outstretched wings while attempting to shift its balance. The view of the underside of the wing shows off the primaries, secondaries, and axillars, or "armpit" feathers.

Pay attention to the arc of the tail feathers, and also to how far forward the leg is in relation to the body.

Close-up of the left flank feathers and leading edge of the left wing. Note the edge of the primary covert feather at the top.

Feathering of the left foot is hairlike. The fleshy pad of the inside toe is clearly visible, revealing reptilian scales and bumps.

Observe the folded left wing primary feather group and outer portion of the left foot.

FRANK MCMAHON

The clenching power of the foot is obvious on this thick leather glove.

FRANK MCMAHON

The appearance of the juvenile's feet is quite different from that of the adult's. Also, see how pronounced the beak is in relation to the head before the development of facial fluff.

FRANK MCMAHON

Back view of a three-week-old great horned owl.

FRANK MCMAHON

The older, dominant chicks are standing about the others in anticipation of their next meal. The chick on the lower right appears to have an injured right eye. This condition is not uncommon among large groups of nestlings due to the long period of close proximity and dangerous weaponry.

FRANK MCMAHON

A hungry cluster of eyes, snapping beaks, and fluff.

FRANK MCMAHON

A happy family portrait. Note that the ear tufts are just beginning to develop on some of the birds.

A nice range of head positions can be seen in this series of side views. It's interesting to note that some adult great horned owls have distinct heavy barring on the upper tail, and others, like the one pictured here, do not.

NON-EARED OWLS

BOREAL OWL
Aególius funéreus

NORTHERN HAWK OWL
Súrnia úlula

SNOWY OWL
Nýctea scandíaca

GREAT GRAY OWL
Stríx nebulósa

NORTHERN PYGMY-OWL
Glaucídium gnóma

ELF OWL
Micrathéne whítneyi

NORTHERN
SAW=WHET OWL
Aególius acádicus

COMMON BARN OWL
Týto álba

BURROWING OWL
Athéne cuniculária

SPOTTED OWL
Stríx occidentâlis

BARRED OWL
Stríx vária

Northern Saw-whet Owl
Aegolius acadicus

How did this owl receive its odd name? There are many colorful stories of an old logger filing his saw and hearing a similar chortling whistle coming from the surrounding spruces only to discover the mimic to be a 7 1/2-inch-tall feathered "teddy bear." The real story probably originated along the U.S.-Canadian border back in the late 1700s or early 1800s. This tame and approachable little owl was a common woodland visitor to camps and farms—probably attracted by the abundance of insects and rodents drawn by lights and stored food. French culture and language were widespread throughout the Canadian wilderness, and the French word for a small owl is *chouette* (pronounced *shoo-ET*). As encounters with English-speaking Americans became more common, it's easy to see how *chouette* became Anglicized into saw-whet.

With a range extending throughout most of the North American continent, with the exception of the desert Southwest, this tough little hunter prefers nesting in abandoned flicker holes in mixed softwood forests, usually near water. Prey consists of a large variety of insects, mice, bats, and small songbirds. Nighttime is when saw-whets seem to be most active, but it has been well documented that a wide range of diurnal prey factors heavily in their diet. The saw-whet's flight pattern is similar to that of a woodcock, giving it an erratic but highly maneuverable flight and enough speed to catch its prey on the wing.

Large yellow eyes seem to give the owl a look of perpetual curiosity and add greatly to its visual appeal. Fledglings look nothing like adults. They have a soft, almost furlike quality and are solid tan or brown, with a bright white V over the eyes. For many years, juvenile saw-whet owls were thought to be a different species altogether.

SPECIES PROFILE

1. This small, 7- to 8-inch earless owl is one of the better-known owls because of its approachable, tame nature.
2. Its name is derived from the French word *chouette,* meaning "little owl."
3. Feeds on a wide variety of small rodents and songbirds.
4. Males and females are plumaged identically, but females tend to be a bit larger and heavier.
5. The bright yellow eyes are topped off with fluffy white brows, giving this owl an endearing, friendly look.
6. Nests in tree cavities and occasionally accepts man-made nest boxes.
7. Highly nocturnal; roosts during the daylight hours.
8. Juvenile saw-whet owls look like an entirely different species, lacking any white spots and being solid brown overall.
9. Its little feet are densely feathered right down to the toes, which are tipped with needlelike talons.
10. The head and nape area on adults is covered with fine white spots that become much more crowded around the outer edges of the facial disks.

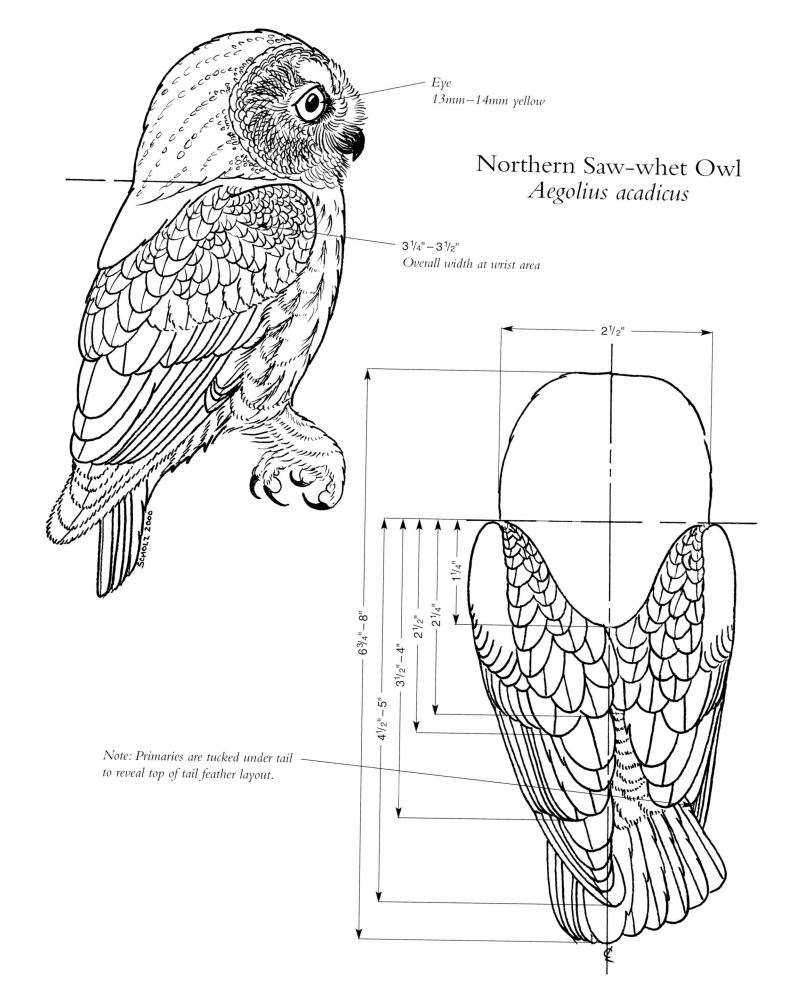

Eye
13mm–14mm yellow

Northern Saw-whet Owl
Aegolius acadicus

3¼" – 3½"
Overall width at wrist area

2½"

1¼"

2¼"

2½"

3½" – 4"

4½" – 5"

6¾" – 8"

*Note: Primaries are tucked under tail
to reveal top of tail feather layout.*

SCHOLZ 2000

The look that endears the saw-whet owl to so many is captured here.

The front area, which includes the beak, eyes, and facial disk, makes up exactly one-half of the overall head depth.

See the wonderful flow established by the white spots. Notice that the spots appear brighter, smaller, and in much greater concentration around the outer perimeter of the facial disk.

The sharply hooked beak is black, and the eyes are encircled by black feathers.

The white, fluffy, gossamerlike eyebrows are clearly shown. Note the shape and structure of the tiny white streaks as they spray up and away from the forehead.

As the black markings expand away from the eyes, they seem to disperse in a herringbone pattern.

This curious saw-whet owl is looking back over its shoulder. Notice that the two distinct white spots under the beak follow the overall head movement.

This view of the back of the head down to the outer edge of the scapular feathers shows that the white markings get softer and much more subtle.

The white "bow tie" under the beak creates a distinct line of transition above the soft breast feathers.

Pay careful attention to the shape and structure of the fluffy pineconing of the ruffled feathers under the beak region. Note that the lower rims of the facial disks hook upward to connect with the lower portion of the rictal bristles surrounding the beak.

A clear view of the feather structure making up the contour feathering of the head.

This macroview of the facial disk clearly illustrates the shape and interplay of the facial disk feathering. These highly specialized feathers are designed to direct sound waves back to the ear openings on either side of the head.

Those needle-sharp talons come in handy when it's time to eat.

This view of the folded wing shows off all the major flight feathers and provides a good look at the foot.

Primaries, primary coverts, secondaries, secondary coverts, and the tail.

Same view as the preceding photo, but notice the radical change in the look of the primaries as they are tightly folded, revealing much more of the upper tail surface.

Dynamic furlike feathering covers the upper wing section as this owl leans forward and turns its head. Notice the pronounced alula feathers at the bottom of the wing edge.

A forward-leaning pose filled with anticipation. Look at the concentration of heavy rippling that occurs on the inside vanes of the primary wing feathers.

A cute little owl.

Opposite page: Soft convergence of three distinct feather groups—head feathers, scapulars, and upper wing (patagial) feathers.

A highly animated pose of an adult saw-whet owl. Notice how the feather groups all relate to one another and the minimal amount of feather deflection in the upper chest area, despite the radical turning of the head.

Curiously, only the outer side of each individual feather is completely white on this outer row of scapular feathers. Many owls have a distinct line of white feathers delineating the outer edge of the scapulars.

A gnat's-eye view of the preceding photo showing complexity and depth.

Opposite page: This frontal view shows more of the breast and belly.

Top view of a fully extended wing of an adult saw-whet owl.

When you isolate the tips of the primary feathers, you can see the sawtooth edges of the outermost feathers, an adaptation for silent flight. It's curious that only the first five feathers have white spots along the outermost edges.

The underside of an open wing shows a drastic shift in color and texture from the top of the wing. Notice the predominance of white spotting throughout the area.

An extreme close-up of the tip of the wing.

The underside of the secondary feathers, twelve in total.

This view gives an idea of scale.

An interesting juxtaposition of wings creates a cyclonic twist to the overall bird.

A good compositional study of an owl in motion. Notice the flared alula feathers on the upper edge of the wing.

This photograph, taken one second after the preceding one, affords a good open-tail view and leg position.

An isolated view of the top surface of a folded tail.

In this saw-whet owl foot, feather bunching is caused by the leather jesses worn around the legs.

A detailed look at the toes, especially the surface texture of the fleshy pads under the toes.

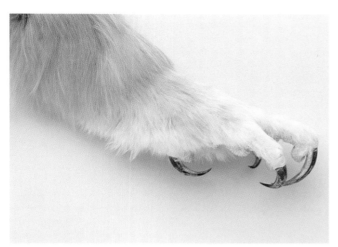

Is this a deadly rabbit's foot? It wouldn't bring much luck to the hapless mouse caught in its grip. Note the thick, dense feathering all the way down to the toes.

The legs extend and join the body quite far up in the belly area. Belly feather flow is beautifully illustrated.

Elf Owl
Micrathene whitneyi

This miniature feathered titan calls the desert Southwest its home. At a height of $5^1/_2$ inches, the elf owl is the smallest owl in North America and has to be mighty tough and resourceful to thrive in such a hostile environment. In the face of temperatures that commonly reach a blistering 110 to 115 degrees, the elf owl has evolved into a solely nighttime hunter. This wise little owl roosts in dense cover, trees, cacti, or other cool hideouts during the day. To avoid alerting any observant adversaries, it rarely roosts and nests in the same location.

Its diet consists of many insects, such as grasshoppers and crickets, formidable scorpions, all sorts of spiders, and even large centipedes, which can almost equal the owl in length. Moths, beetles, and some reptiles round out the menu. Surprisingly, due to their exclusively nocturnal habits, these birds are rather noisy fliers, apparently not needing stealthy silence to grab a late-night snack.

The elf owl is closely associated with the giant saguaro cactus, and until recently, it was thought that these owls were not capable of nesting anywhere else. However, current research shows that they also take up residence in abandoned tree cavities and heavily tangled cottonwood thickets.

These little predators are quite attractive. Their large, round yellow eyes are framed by a perfect sphere-shaped head and trimmed with crescent-shaped white eyebrows. The facial disk is buff to reddish brown. The legs and feet appear disproportionately large in relation to body size, and the short tail is barely noticeable when these birds are perched among the red blossoms of a saguaro. They have 14- to 15-inch wings.

SPECIES PROFILE

1. Small, noneared, rust-colored owl 5 to 6 inches tall.
2. Closely associated with its favorite nesting location—hollowed-out saguaro cactus. Relies on woodpeckers and flickers to excavate the nesting chambers.
3. Diet consists of a variety of insects and small reptiles, occasionally small mice.
4. Total nocturnal activity; rarely flies during the day.
5. Two to four eggs are laid between March and June.
6. Voice consists of myriad chirps, yips, and rising and falling chatterlike staccato yelps.
7. Bright yellow eyes give the bird an endearing presence.
8. Migrate seasonally within their range.
9. Commonly found in canyons and deserts.
10. Frequently found at elevations from 3,000 to 5,000 feet.

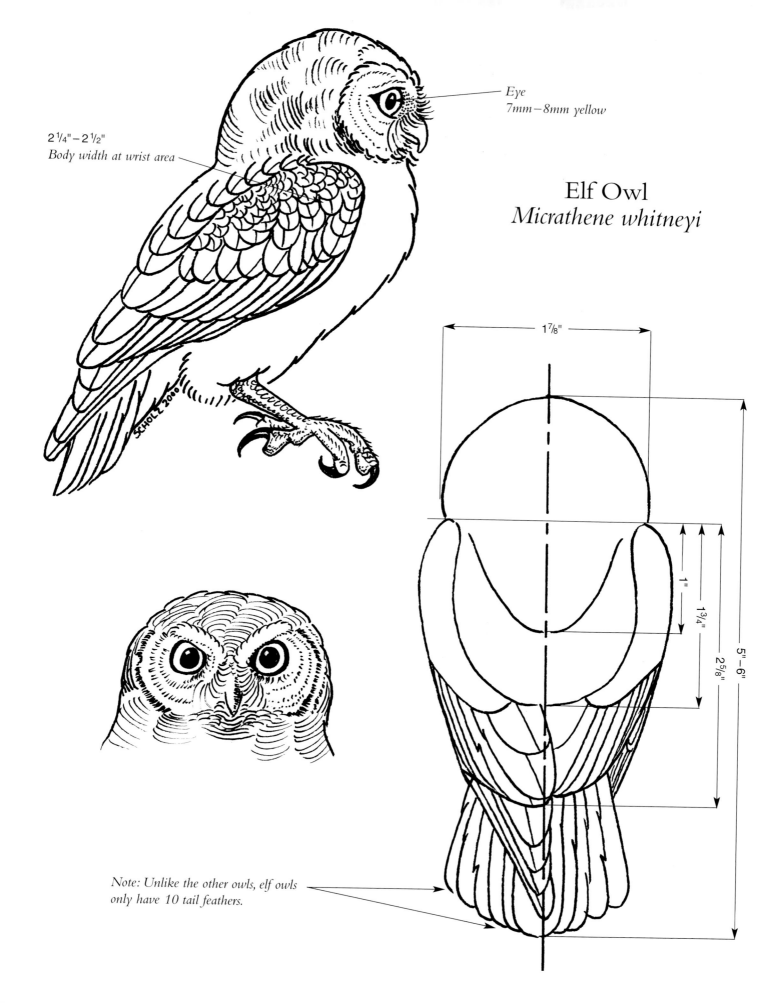

Eye
7mm–8mm yellow

2¼"–2½"
Body width at wrist area

Elf Owl
Micrathene whitneyi

SCHOLZ 2000

1⅞"

1"

1¾"

2⅝"

5"–6"

Note: Unlike the other owls, elf owls
only have 10 tail feathers.

This front view shows off the head-to-body proportions. In relation to body length, the wings are quite long, as evidenced by the height of the upper wrist, strongly edged in white.

FRANK MCMAHON

FRANK MCMAHON

Good feather flow and feather group relationships are shown in this side view. The scapulars are edged in white. Also notice the eye-to-beak relationship.

FRANK MCMAHON

With eyes fixed in their sockets, extreme head mobility is essential for a wide field of view.

FRANK MCMAHON

Faint spots and light streaks can be seen on the top of the head as this little dynamo focuses on something below.

FRANK MCMAHON

This striking, alert pose reveals the large, long legs. Light hairlike feathering extends partially down the legs.

Tight, deep brown barring is offset by softer browns throughout the back and upper wing feathers.

FRANK MCMAHON

A great view of neck extension and feather flow off the back of the head onto the body.

FRANK MCMAHON

This top view of a partially opened left wing reveals the extreme size and development of the secondary feathers. Notice the bright white triangular barring on the number 2, 3, 4, and 5 upper primary feathers.

FRANK MCMAHON

Reaching way over and preening its back, this little elf owl gives us a good look at the directional layout of its belly, chest, and breast feathers. They appear more furlike than featherlike.

Look at the shape, color, and size of the feet. Also, check out the beautiful feather dynamics along the primary coverts and primaries (along the edge of the wing).

FRANK MCMAHON

FRANK MCMAHON

An almost nonexistent facial disk region appears around the eye.

The upper wrists extend almost all the way up to the eye area. These little hunters have an extraordinary flight capability, obvious by the size and development of the wing.

FRANK MCMAHON

FRANK MCMAHON

A line of spots trails up the secondary coverts.

The two bright white wing linings are distinctive.

FRANK MCMAHON

The prominence of the nostrils and beak is evident. Also note the brightness in those eyes.

FRANK MCMAHON

This back view with partially flared wings gives a detailed look at feather patterning, tertials, and the movement of the neck feathers as the bird turns its head.

FRANK MCMAHON

A moody, contemplative downward gaze.

FRANK MCMAHON

Look at the gentle arc of the leading edge of the wing as it glides down to the underside of the tail.

Notice the tip of the beak buried in the upper wing in this strong profile view.

FRANK MCMAHON

For their size, these owls have very long toes.

Wings are drawn into the body a bit tighter as the mood of this bird changes.

FRANK MCMAHON

FRANK MCMAHON

It's amazing how body dynamics can change. This owl stretches up to appear taller.

FRANK MCMAHON

This is a great profile look at the head and beak.

FRANK MCMAHON

A revealing view of the upper leg and how it inserts into the body.

FRANK MCMAHON

Cascading off the back of the head, the feathering opens up, creating a scalloped effect.

FRANK MCMAHON

An interesting perspective of an elf owl clutching a vertical surface.

FRANK MCMAHON

Stretching upward, this bird assumes a barn owl–like leg stance.

FRANK MCMAHON

Observe the small, stiff feathers shooting out from under the beak. This area is not often seen in such detail, especially on an elf owl.

This elf owl looks like he means business. Note the good eye-to-beak view.

This owl is opening up its wings a bit, almost like an upright threat display. Note the knock-kneed position of the legs.

FRANK MCMAHON

FRANK MCMAHON

A lot of useful information can be gathered from this view of the back of the legs and undertail covert feathers.

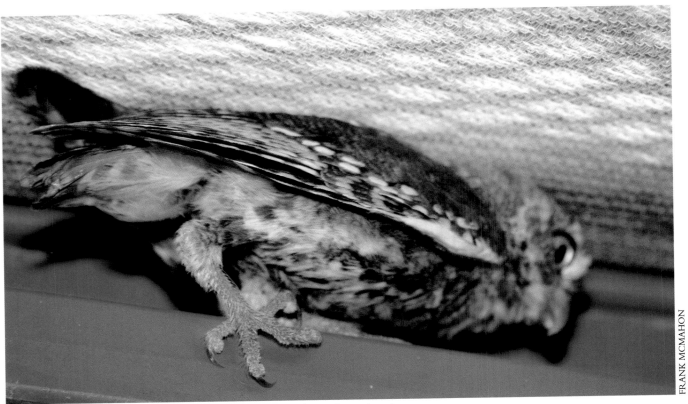

FRANK MCMAHON

The foot assumes an almost crablike grip on the perch as this owl crouches down.

Opposite page: A tall, thin, demure pose for the camera. FRANK MCMAHON

Pygmy-Owls

Due to their extreme similarity in size, plumage, and lifestyle, I combined the species information on the ferruginous pygmy-owl and the northern pygmy-owl.

FERRUGINOUS PYGMY-OWL (*GLAUCIDIUM BRASILIANUM*)

The ferruginous pygmy-owl, so named because of its coloring and small size, can vary considerably from bright rufous and chocolate brown to dull gray and white mottled patterns. The long tail is marked with seven to eight dark crossbars and is rust colored on top. Another noticeable plumage pattern found on most of the pygmy-owls is two distinct, dark eyespots on the back of the head. These "false eyes," as they are called, may have evolved as a warning or to fool the enemies of this small owl. They turn their heads astonishingly fast, and one could get the impression that these birds have two faces.

Although most active at dusk and dawn, the ferruginous pygmy-owl is one of the most diurnal of owl species. It is not uncommon to see one out and observing the landscape for its next meal. Apparently, this owl doesn't realize that it is small and does not hesitate to attack and feed on animals up to twice its size and weight. It has the ability to outfly and catch hummingbirds on the wing. This owl has also been observed attacking large rats snakes and even attempting to overcome and kill a weasel. However, in that case, the owl's eyes were much bigger than its stomach, and it became the weasel's dinner.

NORTHERN PYGMY-OWL (*GLAUCIDIUM GNOMA*)

This western cousin of the ferruginous pygmy-owl is the same size and shape. The visual difference between the two occurs in the color and patterns of the plumage. The northern pygmy-owl has tiny white spots all over its head; a long, perky, white-barred tail; and a much greater concentration of vertical streaks on its underparts than the ferruginous pygmy-owl.

When perched in a tree, the northern pygmy-owl has a habit of pumping its tail like a shrike. These owls live and nest in the vast pine forests of the Pacific Northwest, usually occupying vacant woodpecker cavities and occasionally evicting the tenants in a bloody fight. Bird-watchers keen to observe a northern pygmy-owl in the wild are sometimes tipped off by the angry racket of the resident songbirds mobbing and scolding the indifferent predator.

SPECIES PROFILE

1. Very small (6 to 7½ inches) with bright yellow eyes and a small, nondeveloped facial disk with no ear tufts.
2. Mostly diurnal in its habits; a swift and deadly predator.
3. Voracious hunter that preys on a wide range of species, from small insects to rodents, gophers, and birds the size of a grouse.
4. Males and females are virtually identical in plumage, with females being perhaps slightly larger.
5. Ranges of both pygmy-owls are restricted to the westernmost parts of the United States and Mexico.
6. Nests in a wide variety of situations, from tree cavities to abandoned squirrels' nests and holes in saguaro cacti.
7. The yellow-colored beak is large in relation to head size.
8. The head is fairly big in relation to the body, and the long tail is typically barred in white.
9. The chief physical differences between the two pygmy-owls are the subtle coloring and number of bars on the tail. The ferruginous pygmy-owl has up to ten white bars on its tail and is usually a sienna brown, whereas the northern pygmy-owl may be slightly larger and never has more than eight bars on the tail.
10. Both pygmy-owls possess the distinct eyespots on the back of the head.

Northern/Ferruginous Pygmy-Owl
Glaucidium gnoma/brasilianum

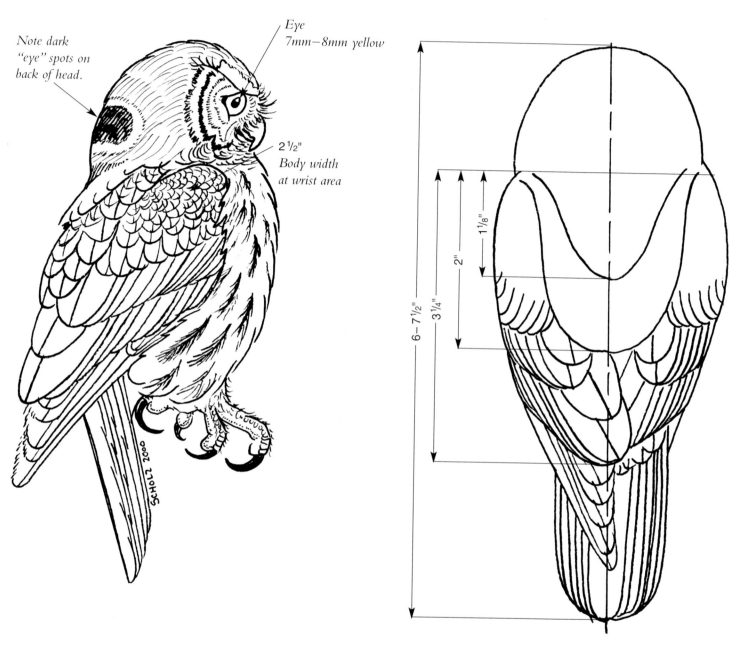

Note dark "eye" spots on back of head.

Eye
7mm–8mm yellow

2½"
Body width
at wrist area

6–7½"

3¼"

2"

1⅛"

SCHOLZ 2000

Text continued from opposite page

These owls are quick and agile fliers and have little trouble overcoming prey, be it feathered or furred. Another good name for the pygmy-owls could be accipiter owls, as they seem to be round-headed, fat, yellow-eyed versions of a sharp-shinned hawk.

One interesting characteristic is the northern pygmy-owl's preference for preying on other birds while it is nesting and raising its young. One tough lit- tle northern pygmy was witnessed attacking and attempting to kill a grouse many times heavier and larger than itself. Often they kill their next meal only to find that it is too big and heavy to carry off to a perch.

Northern pygmy-owls do not mind snow and cold weather. They do not migrate—the exception being those found in the rugged mountains, which drift to lower regions when the weather turns fierce.

163

VERN HESKETH

VERN HESKETH

Front view of the face of a northern pygmy-owl shows the undeveloped facial disk and heavy spotting throughout the front of the head.

The yellow beak is large in relation to overall head size.

VERN HESKETH

This little dynamo is covered in the remains of its last meal.

Side view of a perched northern pygmy-owl shows its long tail and relatively large yellow feet.

VERN HESKETH

A pair of northern pygmy-owls perched at a rehabilitation center.

VERN HESKETH

Note the eye angle and frequency of subtle spots throughout the head.

VERN HESKETH

The stark white belly and breast areas are streaked with bold, dark brown markings arcing vertically toward the center of the front.

This northern pygmy-owl's small size is evident as it perches on the fingers of its handler.

VERN HESKETH

VERN HESKETH

Close-up view of the lower belly feathering and the powerful, intimidating feet.

VERN HESKETH

Opposite page: A good look at the belly and flank feathering and the size, shape, and color of the feet and talons. VERN HESKETH

The upper chest area is more solidly colored and lacks the distinctive streaking found below.

VERN HESKETH

A pair of perching northern pygmy-owls.

Good toe positioning and head-to-body proportion are visible in this full profile view.

Notice the extreme shift in feather color and design from the belly region up to the outer and central breast area.

A nice resting pose.

VERN HESKETH

VERN HESKETH

VERN HESKETH

A good look at the well-developed and sharp weaponry.

A revealing look at the long, heavily barred tail and upper tail covert feathers.

VERN HESKETH

Note the dramatic toe positions.

A pleasing line follows the arc from the back of the head to the tail.

VERN HESKETH

Straight-on head profile shows a well-developed eyelid structure and eye-to-beak proportion.

FRANK MCMAHON

VERN HESKETH

Lower three-quarter front view of a scrappy little predator.

FRANK MCMAHON

A curious little northern pygmy-owl looks downward.

FRANK MCMAHON

Eye angle is shown.

Back view shows good folded wing layout and the distinct outer edging of the scapular feathers.

FRANK MCMAHON

Good eye-to-beak proportion and color.

FRANK MCMAHON

Widely spaced eyes are separated by white patches of eyebrow feathering.

Distinct dark stripes and large, powerful, clutching feet are apparent. Note how the talons converge into one another when the foot is tightly clutched.

FRANK MCMAHON

FRANK MCMAHON

Top view of an open wing shows the distinct patterning and various intensities of white barring and spotting throughout the major flight feathers of the wings.

Close-up look at side feathering and head shape of a northern pygmy-owl. Notice the extremely fine white spots scattered about the feathers.

FRANK MCMAHON

FRANK MCMAHON

The underside of an open wing reveals tightly regimented bright white spots, closely resembling the wing of an American kestrel.

FLOYD SCHOLZ

Pygmy-owls, elf owls, burrowing owls, and great horned owls lay claim to breathtaking territory, such as the South Rim of the Grand Canyon.

RON AUSTING

This beautifully proportioned side view of an adult ferruginous pygmy-owl clearly illustrates the balance point: head and upper chest region above and slightly in front of the midpoint of the feet. Note the graceful flow of flank feather markings as the feathers cascade downward and then sweep upward under the wing. Also notice the fluffy, furlike undertail coverts and the slightly cocked tail position.

RON AUSTING

Fantastic leg positions and frontal feather flow are evident in this photo. The large yellow eyes are surrounded by just a hint of facial disk development. Also note the large beak in relation to head size.

Burrowing Owl
Athene cunicularia

Of all the owls in the world, the burrowing owl is most often seen by humans due to its daytime activities and colonial family groups. These 10-inch-tall, long-legged terrestrial colonizers of the southern prairies are probably rivaled only by the saw-whet owl in their appeal.

Much folklore surrounds the burrowing owl's habitat-sharing with prairie dogs and rattlesnakes. Burrowing owls do inhabit the abandoned tunnels and cavities excavated by prairie dogs, but the two species rarely coexist. And a burrowing owl would not think twice about dining on a tasty baby prairie dog. There have been observations of a prairie dog and burrowing owl scrambling in terror into the same cavity when threatened by a patrolling ferruginous hawk or a hungry coyote, but this is survival instinct rather than a particular attraction to or tolerance of each other. If a burrowing owl feels threatened when hiding in its burrow, it can mimic the rattle of a prairie rattlesnake.

The burrowing owl feeds on a wide variety of animals, but insects make up a large portion of the diet. It is viewed as a beneficial species due to its developed taste for scorpions and locusts, but this has led to a decrease in population as a result of agricultural pesticide use.

Adult burrowing owls are soft brown on the back of the head and back and a sandy tan color on the underparts. They have a distinct white throat patch, and bright white eyebrow markings frame their luminescent yellow eyes, ever vigilant for approaching danger or the next meal. The long legs are tightly feathered right down to the toes. Because of this owl's terrestrial nature, the talons are not sharply hooked and are seldom relied on to dispatch prey.

With fast, fluttering wing beats, burrowing owls are powerful fliers, but they would much rather scurry about than take to the air. Their habit of bobbing up and down when agitated has earned them the nickname of the "howdy-do owl" by cowboys and ranchers, as these curious birds seem to be wishing them a good day.

Although these owls are diurnal in their hunting and socializing habits, they can be quite active at nighttime. Recently, researchers compiled detailed accounts of prolonged vocalizations throughout the night, especially before and during courtship and breeding season.

Burrowing owls nest and rear their young in abandoned tunnels excavated by mammals. The main chamber where the clutch is laid tends to average 10 feet or deeper underground. It is not uncommon to find the entrance to an active burrowing owl tunnel piled with the discarded legs and inedible parts of grasshoppers and other insects.

SPECIES PROFILE

1. Small, brown-legged owl that stands about 8 1/2 to 10 inches tall.
2. Most active at daytime, but can be up all night.
3. Commonly found in family groups; considered a colonial nester.
4. Range extends from the central United States westward and south.
5. Feeds on a variety of small animals but prefers grasshoppers and other medium-sized insects.
6. When threatened, can emit a sound like a rattlesnake.
7. Large, luminescent yellow eyes fill up the rather small, undeveloped facial disk.
8. Strong and fast fliers, but prefer to hop and run.
9. Can be very aggressive, especially toward other animals when guarding its burrow and young.
10. Comical habit of bobbing up and down and nodding its flat-topped head led to its nickname "howdy-do owl."

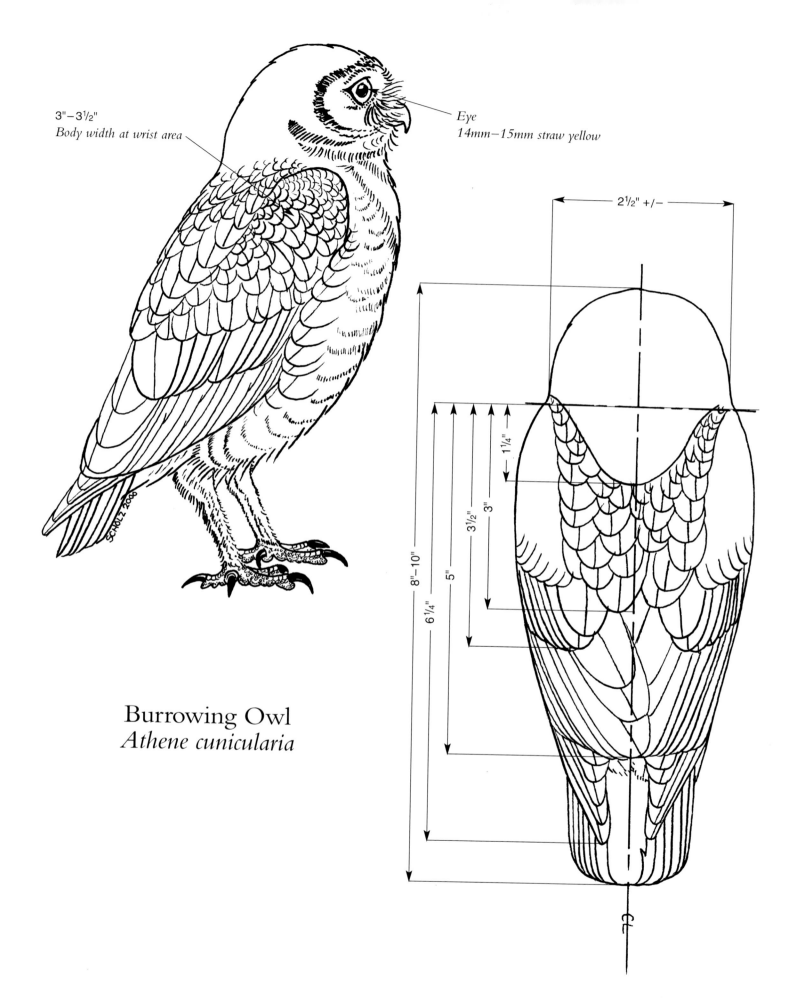

3"–3¹/₂"
Body width at wrist area

Eye
14mm–15mm straw yellow

2¹/₂" +/–

1¹/₄"

3"

3¹/₂"

5"

6¹/₄"

8"–10"

CL

Burrowing Owl
Athene cunicularia

SCHOLZ 2000

Extremely large, saucerlike eyes and pronounced beak and nostrils diminish the size of the almost nonexistent facial disk.

This spot-on profile view of the head shows off the eye angle, eyelid detail, and eye-to-beak proportion. Also notice the well-developed rictal bristles, which extend well beyond the front of the beak.

The back of the head looks like blowing, drifting sand. Note the interesting plumage structure, very loose and hairlike.

The scowl of an owl. The fleshy upper eyelids are trimmed in fine feathers along the outer edge.

The relatively small head is set on a cushion of facial ruff that extends across the bottom of the facial disk and beak.

A distinct white neck-band divides the nape and scapular feathers from the head region.

Beautiful feather flow above and around the eyes. Notice especially the forehead area.

Opposite page: The eye structure is mesmerizing. Due to the dusty, desert environment, the eyelids are very well developed, with thick, bushy feathering around the eye.

The beak color changes considerably from the upper region around the cere and nostrils down to the tip.

Great view of the back and major flight feathers. Note that the primary feathers extend almost to the tip of the tail.

No, this bird is not exploding. It's simply realigning its feathers—an action called rousing.

This bird looks up, exposing its throat fluff.

The burrowing owl could be renamed the "prairie spotted owl."

A good study in foot position and balance as this owl looks to one side while leaning forward.

This round, barrel-chested little owl gives us a look at its breast feathers overlapping and splitting onto the upper wing.

Another great foot and leg study. Being terrestrial, these owls have no need for feathering on the legs and toes.

A close-up look at the tip of the tail, primaries, secondaries, and tertials, and especially the feather patterning, with lots of spots and barring.

This little guy is taking a bow for a job well done.

Throughout the back region of a burrowing owl, it can be difficult to distinguish and isolate the various feather groups because of the similarity in feather structure and plumage patterns.

Burrowing owls can vary their body shape considerably—from tall and thin to short and round.

A similar pose, but an altered head position.

If this little owl sat motionless on a pebble-strewn, light-dappled prairie, it would be all but invisible.

Observe the wide range of textures and structures of the complex leg and foot area. Note the curvature and shape of the front talon.

Dry, scaly, skinlike covering extends up the leg to where the leg joins the body. This section is comparable to a human heel.

FRANK MCMAHON

Classic zygodactyl toe formation. Also note the inward directional flow of the larger, softer belly feathers.

A nice head profile and view of the upper edge of the wing. Notice the enlarged pupil, giving maximum light.

FRANK MCMAHON

FLOYD SCHOLZ

The upper chest feathers fully overlap the wrist section of the wing.

A lone burrowing owl at Cave Creek, Arizona, in the desert evening.

The breast area appears to be divided into two distinct sections.

An alert adult burrowing owl.

A classic knock-kneed pose and view of the upper wing position.

This pose shows the burrowing owl's ability to stay low and undetected while sneaking back to the burrow. Notice the heel joint of the leg extending up and beyond the tertial feathers.

Opposite page: Note the patterning and soft brown and white tones found throughout the body of a burrowing owl.

A good balanced pose. Note the angle of the legs as they enter the body.

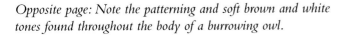

An aerial view of the top of the head, showing the distinguishing white arrow that forms the eyebrows.

FLOYD SCHOLZ

This is typically what a marauding hawk or eagle would see just before this sprinter makes it back to the safety of its burrow.

Common Barn Owl
Tyto alba

There is absolutely nothing common or barnlike about this otherworldly, winged denizen of abandoned structures and lonely woodlots. The finest spun silks and satins pale in comparison to the pearlescent, shimmering, argentine underwings of the barn owl. Moonlight reflected off a silent, undulating silvery-white form spanning three feet across must have certainly provided fodder to the already superstitious overactive imaginations of our ancestors.

From the standpoint of appearance, the barn owl is unmistakable, for it doesn't resemble any other owl. With its long, heart-shaped face, dispassionate dark eyes, and knock-kneed stance, its gangly demeanor belies its stealthy abilities. The barn owl's mastery of locating and catching prey in total darkness is just now beginning to be fully understood. The highly modified bristles and parabolic facial disks direct even the faintest sound to the offset, supersensitive ears. Recent experiments have revealed that the broad vocalizations and clicks emitted while in flight or while hunting could be a form of sonar. Whales, dolphins, and bats employ a similar strategy for finding prey and navigating.

Possessing a fairly short tail and a reasonably small body, the barn owl looks like it is all wings, head, and legs. Those long legs are tightly feathered down to the top of the toes, affording the owl an extralong reach to seize prey hiding in clumps of grass or stacked hay.

The family of barn owls is a large and far-ranging one. Barn owls are found throughout the world and are represented by eleven subspecies, ranging in size from the Madagascar grass owl *(Tyto soumagnei),* about $10^1/_2$ inches tall, to the masked owl *(Tyto novaehollandiae),* about 20 to 21 inches tall. Our North American representative *(Tyto alba)* falls somewhere in between at about 14 to 18 inches. This owl is one of the more challenging subjects to paint because of its soft, subtle coloring, variation in plumage, and ultrafine vermiculations of the back, head, and wings.

One fascinating barn owl behavior is the snakelike waving of its head and extended back-and-forth neck motions when it feels threatened. The suppleness and length of the neck are extraordinary.

Due in large part to their amazing ability to catch mice and rats, the barn owl has been referred to as the most beneficial bird in the world. In some southern Asia plantations, where exploding rat populations are a problem, nest boxes are being installed in an attempt to attract pairs of barn owls. The ability of a growing barn owl to consume mice and rats is legendary, with one subadult bird reportedly swallowing eight mice in a matter of minutes.

SPECIES PROFILE

1. Gangly in appearance, about 14 to 18 inches tall, with golden tan coloring above, pure white or buff white below.
2. Distinct heart-shaped face surrounding two small black eyes.
3. Long, knock-kneed stance gives it a distinct posture.
4. Females tend to be slightly larger and more heavily and darkly patterned than males.
5. Extremely nocturnal, it can locate and capture prey solely by sound.
6. Tail and major flight feathers are darkly barred and interspersed with subtle vermiculations.
7. Diet is almost entirely mice, rats, and other small mammals, although beetles and even reptiles may be eaten.
8. Vocalizations cover a wide array of eerie and sinister sounds, such as rattling chains and blood-curdling screams.
9. Nests in abandoned buildings, grain silos, railroad boxcars, or any quiet space that offers shelter from the elements and ready access to food.
10. Worldwide, one of the most widely distributed birds of prey.

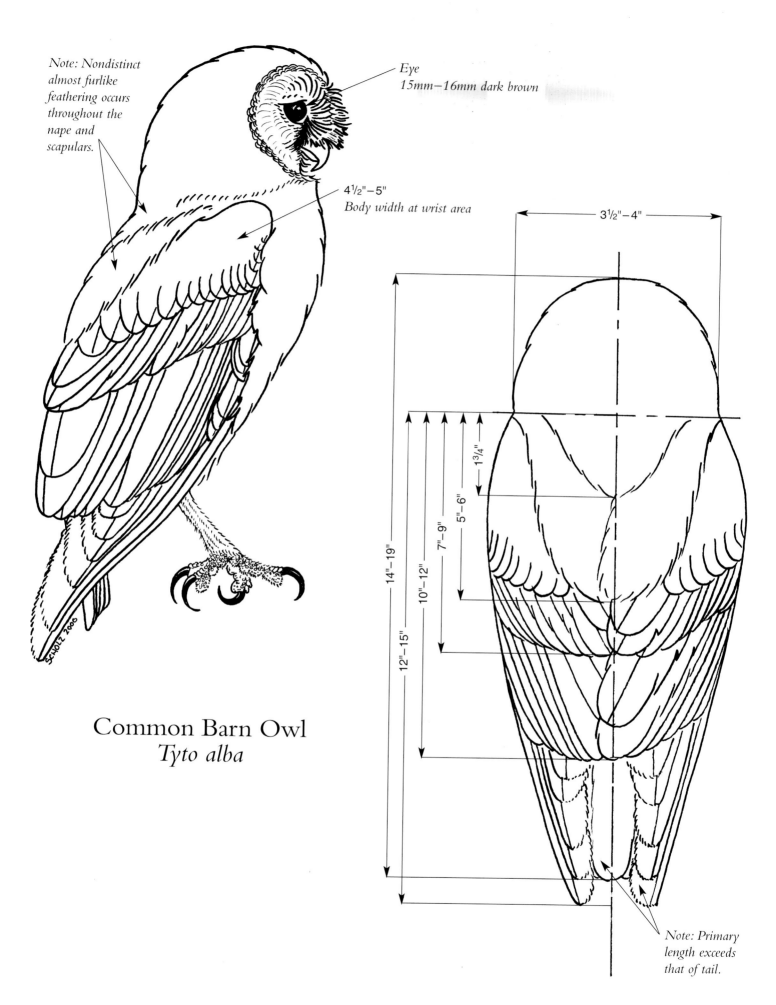

Note: Nondistinct almost furlike feathering occurs throughout the nape and scapulars.

Eye
15mm−16mm dark brown

4½"−5"
Body width at wrist area

3½"−4"

1³/₄"

5"−6"

7"−9"

10"−12"

14"−19"

12"−15"

Common Barn Owl
Tyto alba

Note: Primary length exceeds that of tail.

Upper chest and frontal view of the face clearly show the heart-shaped facial disk that is such a hallmark of this species.

The deep-set eyes are small in relation to the head. The amazing concave shape of the facial disk serves to reflect even the faintest sound waves back to the huge ear cavities located along the outer perimeter. Note the separation of the upper chest feathers and the underbeak ruff.

The pinkish beak is barely visible. It's almost entirely buried in the gossamerlike feathering in front of the eyes.

This close-up of the upper rim reveals its complicated structure.

Transition areas merge as the upper wing softly blends into the upper chest feathering. Note the good head placement.

Females tend to be larger and more distinctly marked.

Extreme mobility enables very little to go unnoticed. Observe how the head feathers react in this position. They move independently of the surrounding feather groups below.

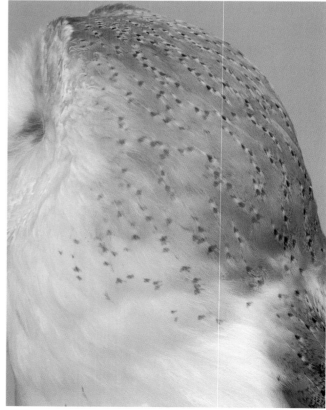

An exceptionally soft, directional flow is evident, with subtle markings on the back of the head.

A nice view of the layout of the major feather groups.

The enormous ear cavities of this nocturnal hunter enable it to locate its prey with pinpoint accuracy, even during the blackest of nights. (Thanks to Bob Fox of Wild at Heart for this revealing insight.)

FRANK MCMAHON

Balance point and body posture shift as the head is stretched outward.

The folded wing shows the subtle transition of color and patterning.

The sharp V shape connecting the eyes to the tip of the beak is clearly revealed.

Opposite page: Something has caught the eye of this ever-vigilant bird. Observe the dramatic positioning of the toes.

With the head thrust back and the wings elevated, this owl is ready for flight. Notice the separation that occurs between the primary and secondary feathers.

Patterning and vermiculations are much more concentrated on the top of the head.

These talons stop mice dead in their tracks.

This back view shows the size and length of the primary feathers, which overlap and extend past the tail.

The scapular feathers and nape feathers are elevated as the owl stretches to look downward.

FRANK MCMAHON

Back view of the flared wings and spread tail. Note the heavily vermiculated end of the tail.

FRANK MCMAHON

The delicate barring is obvious in this isolated upper tail surface of an adult barn owl.

The entire top of an outstretched wing shows the large surface area, enabling a stable and buoyant flight.

FRANK MCMAHON

The underside of an adult barn owl wing shows only subtle barring and coloration on the outermost reaches of the primary feathers.

FRANK MCMAHON

Body posture shifts forward as the owl looks over its shoulder and upward.

Notice the angle and length of the upper leg region as it joins the belly area of this adult owl.

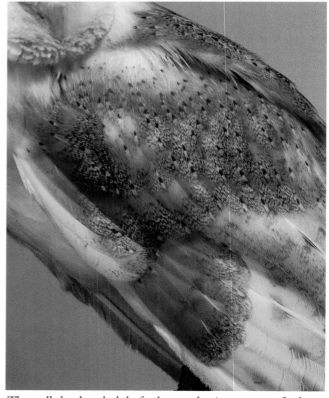

The well-developed alula feathers and primary covert feathers are clearly revealed. Note the fringes along the edge of the lead primary feather at the bottom of the photograph.

As the owl prepares to flare its wings, the entire primary group, primary covert group, and alulae all the way up to the wrist pivot independently of the secondaries, secondary coverts, and upper marginal feather groups.

The cryptic patterning of the upper tail surface.

FRANK MCMAHON

FRANK MCMAHON

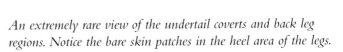

The complexity of the upper wing surfaces and their relationship to the body are clearly illustrated.

An extremely rare view of the undertail coverts and back leg regions. Notice the bare skin patches in the heel area of the legs.

More like fur than feathers, these elevated scapulars meld into the upper wrist of the wing, creating a unified area.

FRANK MCMAHON

The baby owl on the left has a different amount of feathering on its legs than does the much younger one alongside it. Even at this early age, they have the distinctive heart-shaped facial disks.

FRANK MCMAHON

These three barn owls await their next meal. Thanks to the dedication and care of people like Sam and Bob Fox of Wild at Heart in Cave Creek, Arizona, these and countless other birds of prey may have a better chance to survive in a world that seems intent on throwing obstacles in their way.

This highly animated pose clearly shows the placement and insertion point of the open wing. Note the volume of feathers in the front portion of the body and in the downward-sloping tail.

The inner portion of the secondary feather vane is heavily rippled. On an open wing, these ripples would disappear.

This sequence of photos illustrates a variety of body postures and head positions. In terms of artistic reference and general understanding of an animal's personality and mobility, it helps to study its movement and articulation. Keep in mind the extreme importance of balance and symmetry while studying these views. The balance point shifts substantially as the wings are raised and extended, because a majority of the bird's weight is redistributed due to the lifting motion of the underside of the wings and tail. When the head is turned, very little feather deflection takes place under the head itself. Think of the head as a tank turret, revolving independently on its own axis.

Barred Owl
Strix varia

The barred owl is a beautiful medium-to-large bird with a rich brown cloak of feathers that are barred, spotted, and flecked with white over its head, back, wings, and tail. Its chest has horizontal brown and white bars above and ribbons of soft brown streaks throughout its belly and flanks. The barred owl can be distinguished from the other large owl, the great horned, by its lack of ear tufts and its big dark eyes, quite unlike the luminescent yellow eyes of a great horned owl.

This handsome owl is widespread throughout the United States and Canada. It preys on a variety of creatures, including insects, snakes, frogs, fish, grouse, doves, rabbits, and especially rats and mice. It is primarily a nocturnal hunter. The barred owl's vocalizations span myriad sounds guaranteed to give goose bumps to any intrepid nighttime bird-watcher new to the sport of owling. One of the things I look forward to every spring at our mountaintop home in Vermont is the late-night (or early-morning) courtship serenade of the barred owl. I am often jolted from a deep sleep by an enthusiastic *Who cooks for you! Who cooks for you-all!* traded back and forth for hours.

Barred owls prefer to nest in large hollowed-out cavities in old-growth trees. In the north woods and throughout New England, barred owls prefer to nest and live in and around dense stands of mixed evergreens, chiefly spruce, pine, and hemlock. Farther south, they frequent areas that tend to be swampy or are near water, but almost always in close proximity to a deep, impenetrable stand of forest. As more and more old-growth forests are lumbered, barred owls' habitat is quickly dwindling. Unfortunately, they are also frequent victims of speeding cars and trucks. For the most part, barred owls are nonmigratory, preferring to keep to a well-established territory. During the daylight hours, they sleep huddled among thick tangles of branches, relying on their mottled coat of soft brown and white to render themselves invisible.

SPECIES PROFILE

1. One of the most widespread and numerous of the large North American owls.
2. Unpredictable: Sometimes very approachable in the wild; at other times, they spook and fly away at the slightest disturbance.
3. Extremely wide variety of vocalizations, especially during the breeding season.
4. Males and females are plumaged identically, but females tend to be a little larger and heavier.
5. Its name comes from its physical appearance— busy barring all over the head and body.
6. Feeds on a wide range of small mammals, snakes, frogs, small birds, and whatever else it can catch.
7. Cavity nesters, but occasionally raise their young in the abandoned nests of squirrels, crows, or hawks.
8. Large, round eyes are dark and set deeply within the soft gray-brown facial disks, lightly ringed with subtle wavy lines.
9. Nonmigratory; will spend their entire lives within the same territory if food supply and weather permit.
10. When viewed from the front, the long, streaming vertical stripes covering the belly and flank contrast strongly with the tight brown and white horizontal barring of the upper chest.

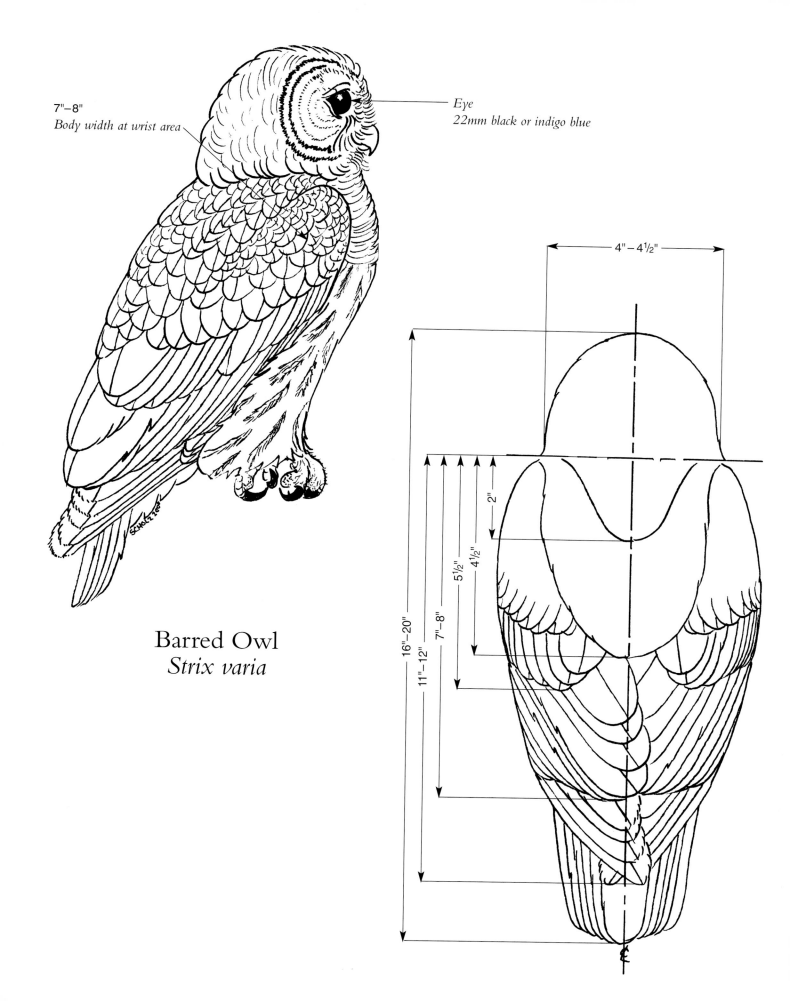

7"–8"
Body width at wrist area

Eye
22mm black or indigo blue

Barred Owl
Strix varia

4"–4½"

2"

4½"

5½"

7"–8"

11"–12"

16"–20"

A straight-ahead view of the head shows the close-set eyes and nicely proportioned beak. Note how the two facial disks are crisply divided above the beak and up onto the forehead.

Deep-set ink-black eyes surrounded by dense feathering give this owl a gentle, nonthreatening look.

A backward glance shows off the deep, dark coloring around the inside half of the eyeball.

A profile view shows the depth and softness of the head. Look at the proportion between the eye and beak, and notice the shape of the rictal bristles that radiate outward from the eyes.

Every filament of feather structure is clearly shown in the upper region of the facial disk.

The dark, hairlike rictal bristles extend quite far from the front of the yellow beak.

Design and color remain constant throughout the head and down onto the breast, shifting abruptly when reaching the belly. Look at the predominance of white feathering under the facial disks.

Good view of the upper corner of the head.

Opposite page: A delicate interplay of soft browns and grays is characteristic of the plumage of an adult barred owl.

The structure of the eyelid is shown. Note the wavering perimeter of the facial disk as it conforms to the upper back area when the head is turned.

The amazingly soft and furlike belly feathers overlap the wing. Note the interplay of disparate feather types.

Another perspective of the lower head area.

Owls can revolve their heads 180 degrees in the blink of an eye.

Back head view showing extremely dense plumage and consistent patterning.

A good overall view of the side of the head.

The nictitating membrane, or "third eyelid," covers the eye diagonally from the inside upper corner.

Opposite page: This owl is hunched over its feet in a characteristic pose.

The long, loose-flowing belly feathers provide a perfect barrier against the cold and wind.

A full back view shows the placement and layout of all the major feather groups. Notice the intensity and shape of the white barring on the tertials and secondaries.

The partially opened tail of an adult barred owl. Count the feathers and see that all twelve are in place.

Good rearward animation.

Close-up of the emarginated primary feathers and ends of the secondary group.

Shifting its weight and extending its wings, this owl is assuming a new pose.

Good geometry of a rearward-looking barred owl. Very little feather deflection occurs as the head is turned.

Upper wing pockets are covered by scapulars on the top and flank feathers on the bottom.

Interesting wing dynamics.

A vast beehivelike area from the top of the head down to the belly.

Wing extension: Observe how well regimented the markings of the secondary feathers are, creating a bold series of white stripes.

The front toes emerge from under the long filaments of belly feathers.

Secondary coverts.

The top tail feather, known as the deck feather.

Underside of the tail, showing the hairy undertail coverts.

Good patterning and separation among the major flight feathers.

I challenge any artist to capture this kind of softness and depth with a tube of paint.

Close-up foot study shows the color and makeup of the dense feathering that covers the legs and toes. Notice the length, color, and shape of the talons.

Another good look at the toes and their positions.

Up close to the transition zone between breast and belly.

Large-format back view of an adult barred owl. The squared-off tertials and secondary feathers are beautifully offset by the gentle arcs of the primary feathers as they overlap the tail.

Cascading flow of head feathers onto the nape area. Note the head-to-body proportions.

The tip of the lower mandible is notched.

This adult barred owl gives us a rare look at his throat, underneath the lower mandible, and even a glimpse inside the soft, pink mouth. This is a view that is almost never seen.

Northern Spotted Owl
Strix occidentalis

This western first cousin to the barred owl is in trouble, with three strikes against it:

1. It is extremely trusting and allows close approach.

2. Its old-growth habitat is being cut.

3. The barred owl has spread westward at an alarming rate in the past thirty years, challenging the spotted owl for precious nest locations and food and, most importantly, endangering its genetic purity. (The two are capable of cross-breeding, which will inevitably homogenize the species.)

Although it is fairly widespread throughout its range, the northern spotted owl needs untouched old-growth forest in which to live and breed. Previously unbroken tracts of virgin forests are now sectioned off and separated by clear-cut areas, creating a patchwork environment that is detrimental to the owl's survival. As of this writing, the northern spotted owl is officially listed as an endangered species.

Very similar to the barred owl in size and plumage, the spotted owl is so named because of the distinct white spots covering its head, back, wings, and tail. Its coloring may be a bit more muted and less contrasting than that of its eastern cousin. The eyes are a deep indigo color and are set into two well-defined facial disks framed by dark reddish brown bands surrounding the face. Its beak is a pale yellow color dusted by stiff black bristles.

Being a strictly nocturnal hunter, this owl can be extremely difficult to locate when it is stoically perched, blending into the surrounding woodland. Studies have shown that flying squirrels and pocket gophers make up a large part of the spotted owl's diet. Few woodland creatures smaller than a rabbit are safe from this owl's powerful feet and needle-sharp talons.

Like barred owls, spotted owls are nonmigratory. Very little is known of their breeding and courtship habits. It can be assumed that they prefer to nest in large cavities in old, dead trees and occasionally take up residence in abandoned hawk's or crow's nests. Ornithologists have recognized four races of the spotted owl, based almost entirely on their geographic location.

SPECIES PROFILES

1. Stands from 14$\frac{1}{2}$ to 19 inches tall.
2. Dark brown, earless owl covered completely with faded white spots that become cleaner and brighter on the head and back.
3. Large, dark eyes are framed within a soft gray-brown facial disk.
4. Females and males are virtually identical in plumage, with females being slightly larger.
5. A wide range of vocalizations, similar to a barred owl.
6. Prey consists of small rodents, frogs, toads, insects, and flying squirrels.
7. Listed as an endangered species.
8. Extremely nocturnal in its habits.
9. Four subspecies are officially recognized, based on slight physical differences and geographic location.
10. When encountered in the wild, can sometimes be approached quite closely due to its trusting nature and infrequent encounters with humans.

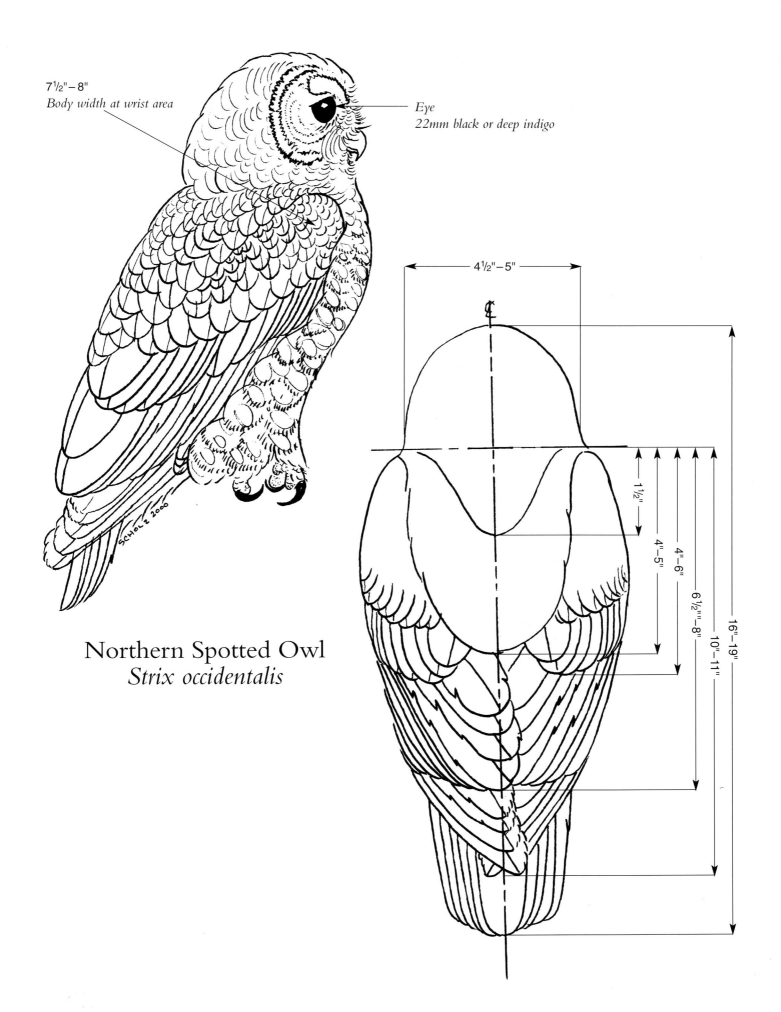

7½"–8"
Body width at wrist area

Eye
22mm black or deep indigo

Northern Spotted Owl
Strix occidentalis

4½"–5"

1½"

4"–5"

4"–6"

6½"–8"

10"–11"

16"–19"

A stunning head profile reveals the shape and depth of the facial disk and the deep brown ruff that surrounds it.

The face and frontal regions of a soft and beautiful old-growth hunter.

Note the patterning of the white spots and the deep russet coloring of the inner feathering along the chest and belly.

A heart-shaped face frames the blinking eyes, which seem to close in two stages—first the nictitating membrane, then the major portion of the lids.

A beautiful array of feathers and soft brown colors. Note the relation of the eyes to the beak.

An adult northern spotted owl.

Opposite page: An interesting study in attitude. VERN AND KAROLYN HESKETH

Notice the furrow that divides the top of the head into two sections.

VERN AND KAROLYN HESKETH

An extraordinary nighttime look at a spotted owl. The white spots really stand out.

VERN AND KAROLYN HESKETH

The purpose of plumage is obvious when the owl is viewed against a dappled sunlit background.

The alula feathers, necessary to stabilize the bird during slow-speed flight, are readily visible. Typically, there are four.

Note the rock-solid stance and interesting folding of the dense head and chest feathers as this owl takes an extreme look backward.

Cascading belly feathers onto and around the feet.

A random collection of white spots, specks, bars, and wavy lines makes up the pattern on the back of this owl.

VERN AND KAROLYN HESKETH

VERN AND KAROLYN HESKETH

A close-up of the scapular feathers and wing area. Note the density of the pineconelike ruff feathers under the beak.

Toes feathered right down to the talons are ideally suited to seize prey.

VERN AND KAROLYN HESKETH

The feather deflection of the leg feathers is caused by the leather jesses worn by the owl.

VERN AND KAROLYN HESKETH

The definitive white bars give way to a subtle blend of nondescript wavy lines as they move up the wing. Also, note the dynamic overlaying of upper chest feathers.

VERN AND KAROLYN HESKETH

Note the series of horizontal brown bars from the base of the toes up the leg.

How sharp these talons are!

An informative look at the breast and belly area. Note the bright white underwing lining.

VERN AND KAROLYN HESKETH

Good view of the lower flank feathers and under the tail. Observe the richness of the browns and the distinct chevron shapes of the undertail coverts.

VERN AND KAROLYN HESKETH

The beak is a translucent yellow color. This view also offers a peek at the pink mouth lining.

VERN AND KAROLYN HESKETH

Variations in brown values occur throughout the secondaries, primaries, and top of tail.

The outer row of scapular feathers exhibits an interesting series of white markings.

VERN AND KAROLYN HESKETH

This is a very serious owl. Notice how the chest feathers seem to bellow outward from under the throat fluff.

VERN AND KAROLYN HESKETH

Soft, luxurious plumage.

VERN AND KAROLYN HESKETH

Front view of an owl leaning forward and looking down. This angle gives a good sense of the cross section of the body. Notice how humped the scapulars appear. Also note the swept-back nature and angle of the eyebrows.

Back view of a dark spotted owl.

Note the distinct isolation of all the major feather groups.

When the head is turned so dramatically, the overall shape assumes an angled, less rounded form.

Opposite page: This northern spotted owl strikes a balanced pose. VERN AND KAROLYN HESKETH

Northern Hawk Owl
Surnia ulula

Believed to be the most highly evolved of all the owl species, the northern hawk owl has good reason to be aloof. It is the sole member of the genus *Surnia,* and as its name suggests, it combines the attributes of other birds of prey. The sum of these parts is a highly refined and efficient hunter and a strikingly beautiful bird.

The northern hawk owl has brilliant yellow eyes in the middle of its delicately textured, soft gray facial disks, framed by two long sideburns of black feathers. The strong downward-sloping eyebrows form a subtle V shape that contributes to the owl's stern look. The top of the beak is pale yellow, and the lower area fades to dark grayish black.

Northern hawk owls are found in the northern-most portions of North America and Europe, preferring to nest and raise their young in the taiga, most often in the vicinity of a bog or other aquatic habitat. Occasionally, however, when food gets scarce up north, these owls delight those of us south of the Canadian border with a visit. I've seen hawk owls on several occasions in Vermont, especially in the Champlain Valley on the western side of the Green Mountains.

They feed almost exclusively on lemmings and other small rodents, but when their favorite dish becomes scarce, they take snakes and birds up to the size of a willow ptarmigan.

They can appear surprisingly kestrel-like when viewed from a distance, and like the kestrel, they hover over open fields while hunting. Hawk owls are diurnal in nature, but early dawn and dusk are the preferred hunting times. These birds are tough and relentless in pursuing prey or defending territory.

Northern hawk owls are extremely fast fliers. Rapid wing beats combine with a long, low, straight flight pattern to more closely resemble the flight of a gyrfalcon or prairie falcon than that of any other owl. Hawk owls are believed to be the fastest of all the owls.

SPECIES PROFILES

1. Overall length 14 to 17 1/2 inches.
2. One of the most undeveloped facial disks of all the owl species.
3. Long tail and semipointed wings are evident in flight.
4. Lemmings, mice, and small- to medium-sized birds make up the majority of food items.
5. Long tail and streamlined appearance make it similar in pose and shape to a peregrine falcon.
6. When the bird is perched in an upright position, the numerous dark horizontal bars are visible from the undertail coverts up to the head, covering the whole frontal region.
7. Probably the most diurnal of all the owls.
8. Smallish, bright yellow eyes are framed by two black sideburns.
9. A cavity-nesting bird that prefers to nest in the vicinity of a muskeg or bog.
10. The top of the dark head is covered with white spots.

Eye
15mm yellow

5¼"–6"
Body width at wrist area

Northern Hawk Owl
Surnia ulula

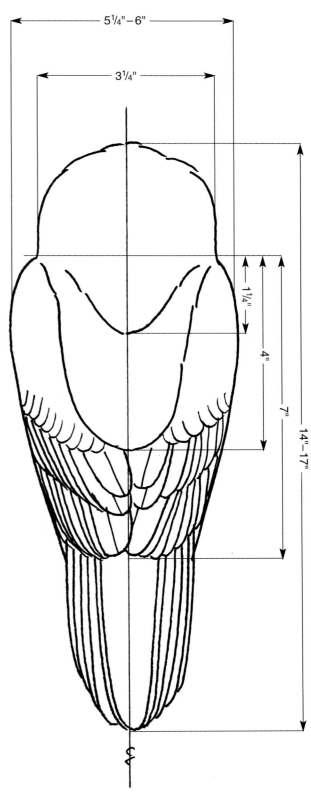

5¼"–6"

3¼"

1¼"

4"

7"

14"–17"

A view of the dark sideburns shows the broken transition line of the outer facial disk and how it overlaps the dark feathers.

The distinct white spots prevalent on the top of the head get longer and blend together as they cascade down the back of the head toward the nape.

The face and head of a northern hawk owl reveal myriad shapes, textures, and plumage patterns. Compared with most other owl species, its facial disks are almost nonexistent.

Opposite page: A rare look at the underside of the beak and overall throat region, showing the feather structure.

The extreme lower back of the head transitions into the nape feathers. Note the shape and texture of these feathers.

As the hawk owl turns its head, an interesting feather dynamic is set up. Notice how the feathers flow out and fan away from the lower corner of the mouth.

The unique dark "goatee" is clearly visible.

The dark face frame extends all the way down to the upper chest feathers. A dark, mottled collar seems to separate the head and throat region from the breast.

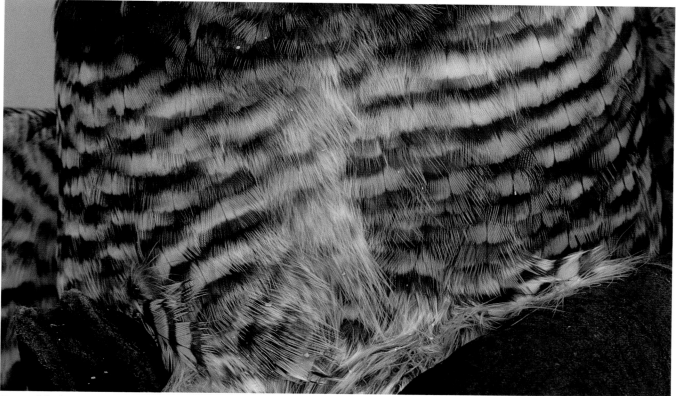

Beautiful, dense chest feathers are highlighted. Note how each feather has a fine, dark centerline.

An extreme close-up of the compact feathering found around the eyelids reveals their structure and color.

This frontal shot shows the symmetry among the profile, chest, and upper wrists of the wings. Also, some talon detail can be seen.

The translucency of the upper mandible and its color are apparent. Pay particular attention to the notches along the upper edge of the lower mandible.

In this open left wing, the clean white spots seem to dominate the outer edges of the tertials, secondaries, and secondary coverts.

The primary coverts of the left wing are isolated. Each has a single white spot located about two-thirds of the way down on the outer edge. Primary coverts typically number ten.

An interesting conglomeration of upper tail coverts, tertials, and right wing secondary coverts.

A fantastic view of the full upper tail surface shows not just the size and shape but also the random nature of the subtle white barring.

The outermost edges of the scapular feathers are trimmed in white, creating a distinct V pattern when viewed from the back.

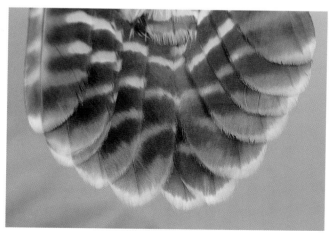

The underside of the tip of the tail reveals a soft transition in color from bright white to soft gray in the distinct barring.

Note the well-developed nature and sharp angling of the undertail coverts as they flow down and cut a V into the tail. The upper part of the undertail coverts turns into a dense mass of nondescript fur.

In the upper chest transition zones, the feathers seem to get shaggier toward the center.

The feather shape, pattern, and structure of the upper wrist area. Notice how it emerges from the overlying scapular feather line.

This close-up of the primary and primary coverts shows the unique shape of the wing, which is best suited for strong, fast, direct flight. Because of its hawklike hunting method, the hawk owl has no need for silent flight, accounting for the lack of hairlike fringes on the front edge of the primary feathers so common in nocturnal owls.

The tips of the right wing primary feathers.

The top forehead region is covered with distinct white spots. Also shown is the spiral flow of the eyebrow feathers.

RON AUSTING

The northern hawk owl typically perches from the highest vantage point in search of prey.

RON AUSTING

This hawk owl strikes a dramatic pose as it cocks its tail high in the air. Note the long primary feathers protruding out back and below.

Something has just caught the attention of this northern hawk owl, always on the lookout for its next meal.

Perched high atop a cedar telephone pole, the hawk owl molds its dense flank feathering to the hard surface, providing a warm, insulated skirt to shield itself from the harsh climate.

A magnificent northern hawk owl in the muskeg area of northern Canada.

Boreal Owl
Aegolius funereus

Ornithological studies suggest that the hardy little boreal owl may be one of the most highly evolved owl species, and it has been endowed with one of the sweetest courtship songs. This attractive bird seems to be well adapted to the harsh environment of the boreal forest—an extreme northern mix of taiga and tundra, characterized by mixed stands of fir, spruce, tamarack, and birch.

This nocturnal owl prowls the dense thickets of spruce bogs that pepper the vast northern taiga. It feeds on small woodland voles and lemmings, with these small mammals accounting for about 90 percent of its diet. As a method of survival in the punishing North, the boreal owl has developed the habit of caching food to be retrieved and consumed later. Food tends not to spoil when the temperature hovers around a balmy −30 degrees Fahrenheit. Although it is known as a lover of the night, in the high arctic, where the sun doesn't set all summer, the boreal owl readily adjusts to daytime pursuits.

Sometimes described as resembling a larger, darker version of the saw-whet owl, the boreal owl has a much more clearly defined facial disk pattern. Its yellow eyes appear even brighter because they are framed in black. Unlike the black beak of the saw-whet, the boreal's beak is pale yellow. Its large head is broad and appears somewhat flat on top. Females can be quite a bit larger than males, but no significant dimorphism exists in plumage.

In North America, this little owl occasionally drifts southward when food gets scarce in its home range and delights bird-watchers along the northern boundaries of the lower forty-eight states. When this bird gets agitated, it has the ability to flare up its crown feathers, forming two distinct horns, but it lacks the well-defined ear tufts of so many other owl species.

SPECIES PROFILE

1. Large head in relation to body size.
2. Fairly small at 8 to 10 inches; sometimes mistaken for a dark saw-whet owl but has much darker streaking throughout the chest and belly.
3. Feeds primarily on small rodents and occasionally northern songbirds.
4. Extremely nocturnal except in the Far North, where the sun never sets.
5. Yellow eyes appear even brighter due to deep, black eye rings.
6. Nesting and egg-laying occur early to coincide with the abundance of lemmings.
7. Cavity nesters, boreal owls take over pileated woodpecker holes or old hollowed-out tree stumps.
8. Their plumage is exceptionally dense and silky, making these little owls appear larger than their actual weight.
9. Quite vocal, especially during breeding season.
10. Distributed worldwide, with all five races found in the extreme northern latitudes.

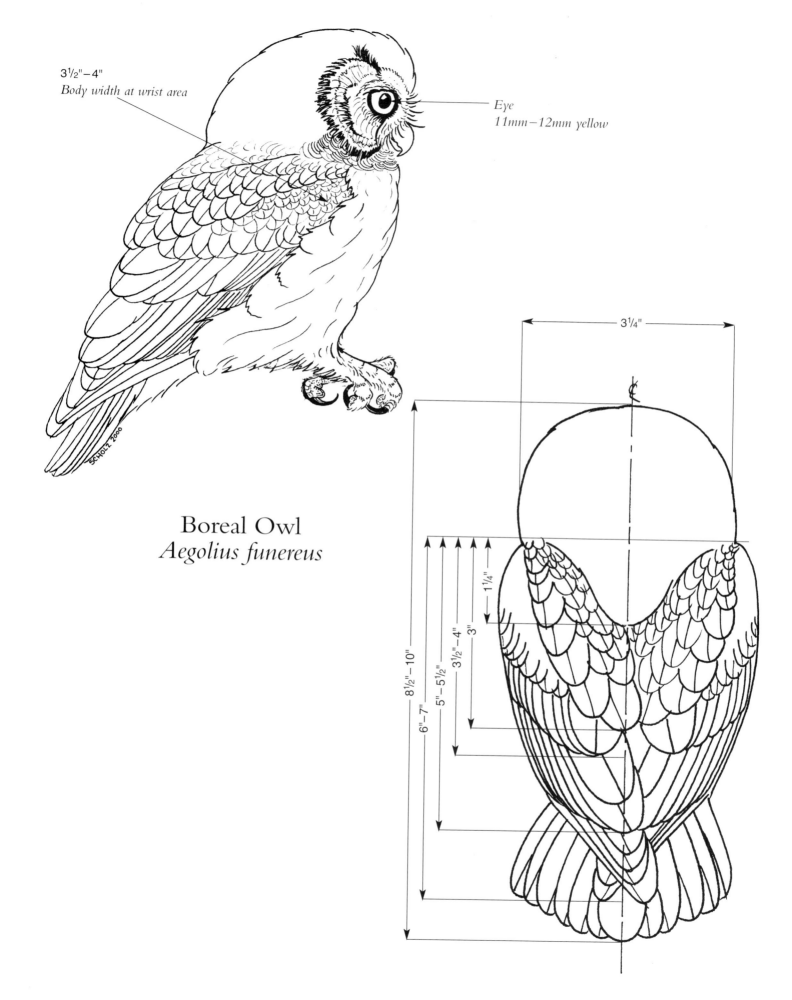

3½"–4"
Body width at wrist area

Eye
11mm–12mm yellow

Boreal Owl
Aegolius funereus

SCHOLZ 2000

3¼"

8½"–10"

6"–7"

5"–5½"

3½"–4"

3"

1¼"

RON AUSTING

A lot of information can be gleaned from this photo. This boreal owl is in its natural surroundings, doing what it does best during the day—resting. It appears slightly annoyed at being photographed, as evidenced by the bulges over the eyes. One foot is drawn up into the body, and the feet appear large in relation to body size, due in part to the dense feathering. Notice the dark bands of feathers flowing off the upper chest down to and around the feet, as well as the distinct polka dots scattered about the forehead.

A wide-eyed adult boreal owl caught by surprise while foraging at night among the boughs of a large hemlock tree.

Strictly nocturnal in its activities, this boreal owl spends the day roosting comfortably among the snowy branches of a spruce tree. Study the colors and textures of the branch and the snow, and notice the similarities with the bird's plumage as it blends with its surroundings.

This female boreal is exploding away from the nest tree in pursuit of her next meal. Note the look of focused intensity in those eyes.

Legs are fully extended and wings outstretched just before contact with the tree.

In its winter roost, this owl is superbly adapted to its environment.

This boreal owl has just returned to its nest cavity with a lemming.

A male boreal owl caught at the entrance of his nest cavity. Note the flow of white spots along the outer edge of the scapular feathers.

ROBERT R. TAYLOR

A great flight study of wing curvature and leg placement.

ROBERT R. TAYLOR

A male boreal is about to return to the nest with a lemming. A solid bite to the neck dispatched this rodent.

ROBERT R. TAYLOR

Great overall view of the underside of an open wing. Look at the shape and position of the facial disk when viewed from the side.

ROBERT R. TAYLOR

An alert owl with its prey perched on the broken stump of a gray birch tree.

ROBERT R. TAYLOR

A female peers out from her nest hole.

ROBERT R. TAYLOR

If you couldn't see the eyes of this female boreal owl, she would virtually vanish into the patterns, colors, and textures of the tree trunk as she peers out from the nest cavity.

ROBERT R. TAYLOR

RON AUSTING

Boreal owls are capable of a wide variety of behavioral poses. Much of an owl's mood and intentions can be determined by its body posture. The owl in this photo exhibits all the outward signs of a perched stance known to experts as an erect concealment posture. The head is slimmed down and the shallow horns are barely evident above the eyes. Also, the right wing is drawn up tightly to the body and the wrist area is level with the beak. Against the trunk of a tree and with its eyes closed, this owl would be extremely difficult to locate.

Snowy Owl
Nyctea scandiaca

Even the casual observer who knows nothing about owls would have little difficulty guessing which part of the world this white powerhouse comes from. In spite of the accolades bestowed on the great horned owl for its strength and size, the snowy owl is in fact heavier and more powerful. Unlike almost all other owl species, there is quite a difference between males and females. Similar to hawks and eagles, the female snowy owl is up to a third larger and heavier than the male. The female is heavily barred throughout the flight feathers, upper wings, back, top of head, belly, and chest. The male is usually pure white or exhibits only light, subtle markings.

Snowy owls nest and raise their young in the Far North. Feeding a hungry, growing family is not an easy task in these barren, windswept areas, but the snowy owl is well equipped to survive. Extremely dense, insulating plumage provides the first line of defense against the elements. The legs and toes are wrapped in thick, furlike coverings that give the feet a shaggy appearance. The beak and talons seem to just barely emerge from dense feathering. The large, glowing yellow eyes are deeply set, with thick, protective eyelids.

These sturdy hunters are most active during the early hours of morning and the dwindling light of dusk, but they are perfectly adept at hunting during the brightest day and the darkest night.

It's not uncommon for vast numbers of snowy owls to migrate south during times of lean food supply or to offset the six months of darkness that envelop the Far North. These so-called invasions become the talk of the town in New England, New York State, and the northern Midwest.

Snowy owls possess amazing powers of flight. A combination of long wings, a long tail, and an extremely powerful build propels this large, ghostlike bird through the air surprisingly fast. Its style of hunting is either to perch motionless on the highest spot around and wait for movement or to cruise low and fast, covering a vast area and hoping to catch a hapless lemming or ptarmigan off guard. It takes quite an array of animals, ranging from geese and seabirds to arctic hares, but its favorite meal is lemmings. Often, mobbing crows or songbirds fall victim to this agile, swift hunter. Credible reports even have snowys dining on carrion when times are difficult.

The snowy owl is truly one of a kind; no other subspecies exist. When they are kept in captivity, they tame remarkably fast and can even become downright affectionate. Jonathan Wood's wonderful snowy owl, Freeze, graces the cover of this book and was the model for this chapter.

SPECIES PROFILE

1. Large, powerful white owl, 19 to 28 inches.
2. Females are larger and more heavily barred than males.
3. Legs and toes are densely feathered out to the talons.
4. Large, bright yellow eyes are set deep within the dense, pure white facial disks.
5. Long wings and tail combined with powerful flight muscles give the snowy owl remarkable flight ability.
6. Tends to roost on the highest vantage point.
7. Most active at dawn and dusk, but can hunt at any time of the day or night.
8. Juvenile snowy owls are substantially darker and more heavily marked than adults.
9. Depending on availability of food, can lay up to fifteen eggs.
10. When viewed from a distance, the head appears small in relation to the body.

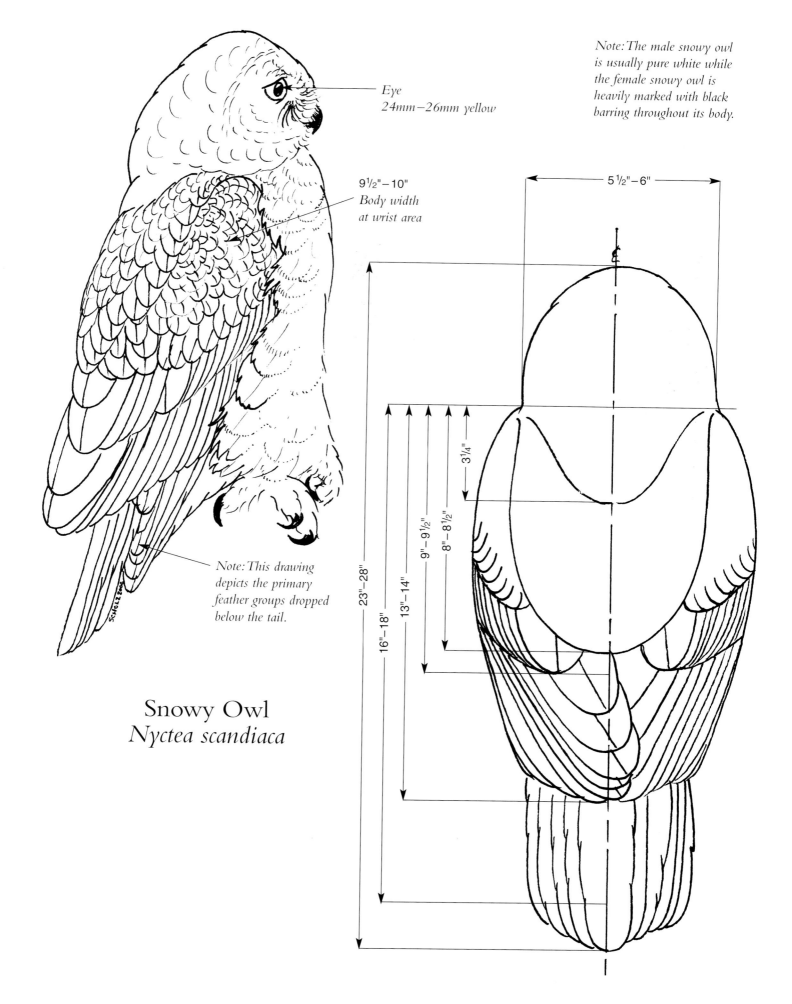

Eye
24mm–26mm yellow

Note: The male snowy owl is usually pure white while the female snowy owl is heavily marked with black barring throughout its body.

9¹⁄₂"–10"
Body width
at wrist area

5¹⁄₂"–6"

3¹⁄₄"

9"–9¹⁄₂"

8"–8¹⁄₂"

13"–14"

16"–18"

23"–28"

Note: This drawing depicts the primary feather groups dropped below the tail.

SCHOLZ 2004

Snowy Owl
Nyctea scandiaca

The extremely dense rictal bristles form a mustache around the upper mandible.

If you've ever wondered what the world's best lemming trap looks like, just take a look. The cavernous mouth seems to divide the head into two parts.

The thick, luxurious throat feathering is evident. Note the gentle sweep of the feathers as they roll off the back of the head and onto the nape.

Note the strong angle of the facial disk and the eye-to-beak proportion.

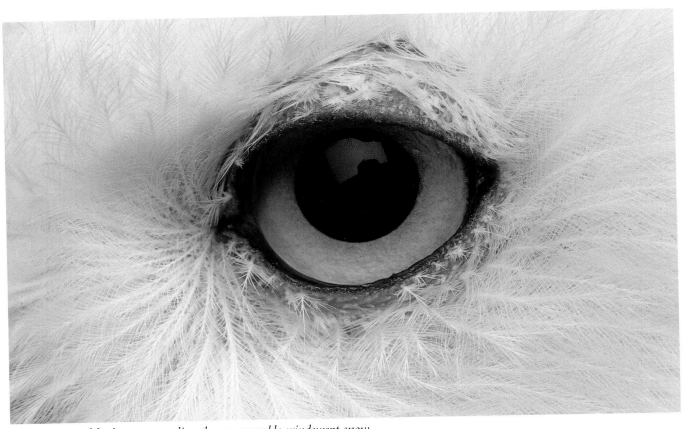

The patterns of feathers surrounding the eye resemble windswept snow.

The facial disk is pure white. On the female owl, the dark markings frame the face.

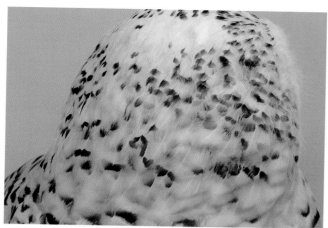

In this close-up of the back of the head, the fine, pure white feather shafts, along with the dark markings, create a beautiful flow.

Four distinct zones are noticeable in this picture: facial disk, rictal bristles, eyebrow area, and bib and throat area.

The delicate, dark markings vary in intensity and size as they softly avalanche away from the outer perimeter of the facial disk. Believe it or not, there's a huge ear opening buried under all those feathers.

Directional flow is amplified by the fine, bright white feather shafts.

Feather transition areas create a real challenge for the artist.

Notice that all the small feathers of the upper chest, belly, and flank areas are beautifully organized and not just placed randomly.

This back view illustrates the mobility of the head and neck.

Very little moves below the turretlike head as the owl looks to one side.

The depth of the molten yellow eyes seems to draw you in.

The scapular feathers are divided into two distinct groups.

A magnificent study of black, gray, and white and how the colors help establish the directional flow of the flank feathers.

Observe the relationship of all the major flight feathers. Pay particular attention to the size and prominence of the well-developed scapular area.

A close-up of the tertials showing the larger bars found in this area.

As the head sharply turns, the breast feathers lightly overlap the upper portion of the wing.

Good foot position.

An avalanche in black and white.

Snowy owls have the ability to completely cover their toes with dense feathering. Notice the length of the feathers that extend past the talons. Remember: Those are highly modified feathers, not hair or fur.

I challenge any abstract expressionist artist to recreate a more dazzling, thought-provoking canvas.

Close-up of the lower belly region.

Notice the translucency of the overlying feathers.

Close-up of the back corner of the head reveals the plush depth of these feathers.

Note the deep-set eye and supple head movement.

The long, emarginated wing-tip feathers enable fast, maneuverable flight. Notice the lack of soft frills on the leading edge of the feathers. Obviously, silent flight is not an issue.

Close-up of the feet showing the stout design and length of the talons.

The soft, white furlike bib covers the upper chest feathers like snow drifts.

The head is small in relation to the body.

This heavily marked female illustrates the well-developed wrist and patagial region of the wing.

Top view of a partially folded wing showing off the long, stiff primary feathers, primary coverts, and alulae. This wing formation is a classic high aspect ratio design.

Top view of a heavily barred female, with a nice look at the top of the tail.

Several wonderful head gesture studies.

Body position can change tremendously, telling a lot about the mood of the owl and what it is about to do. Note the well-balanced foot position.

Great Gray Owl
Strix nebulosa

Based on sheer body size, the great gray is probably the biggest owl in the world. From its oversized fluffy head down to its very long tail, this is one large bird. But outward appearances don't always tell the whole story. If you could strip away all the fluff and feathers, the great gray owl would be smaller and lighter in weight than a snowy owl or a great horned owl.

This is one factor that explains why such a large and imposing hunter limits its prey to small mice and lemmings. It has been known to occasionally eat frogs, insects, and a variety of small songbirds and waterfowl as well.

Worldwide, great gray owls inhabit a vast range, forming a northern band encircling the subarctic regions of the earth. Three subspecies are officially recognized. Calling the dense, forbidding boreal forests and muskeg its home, the great gray is ideally suited to life where deep, drifting snows and unrelenting subzero winds make survival all but impossible for other creatures.

Great grays are extremely aggressive and fearless when defending a nest. Reports abound of unwary naturalists coming away with deep lacerations and blood-soaked clothing to show for their efforts to visit a nest.

I can best describe its facial appearance this way: Imagine if you dropped two golden yellow marbles into smooth, gray water at the same time and the resulting ripples fanned outward in concentric rings. Unlike its neighbor and cousin the northern hawk owl, the great gray owl has a pair of large, perfectly shaped facial disks measuring up to 20 inches across. Proportionately small, pale yellow eyes are set deep in the center of these highly refined parabolic reflectors. As well, the owl's sense of hearing is phenomenal, allowing it to make an aerial strike on a vole, sight unseen, through a foot of snow based on sound alone—with pinpoint accuracy.

There is a considerable size difference between the sexes, with females being larger and heavier. This disparity in size has to do with egg laying and incubation, as well as nest defense and protection of the young from the elements.

Due to their size and weight versus the amount of plumage, the great gray has a buoyant, almost mothlike flight that enables it to navigate through seemingly impenetrable softwood forests. They hunt by perching high up, choosing a vantage point that allows a good field of view, usually bordering a forest clearing or a bog. Always alert for the slightest movement or sound, they glide down, sometimes from up to 300 feet, in pursuit of potential prey.

The long, outstretched legs and large, powerful feet aid in prey acquisition. The talons are large in proportion to the feet and are needle sharp. The beak is a soft yellow color and rests between two distinct white "commas" of eyebrow and stiff rictal bristles.

Due to the remoteness of their home range, occasional nomads that travel southward can be surprisingly approachable, providing the lucky viewer with a chance to experience the physical beauty and size of this "ghost of the north woods."

SPECIES PROFILE

1. Extremely large, long-tailed, big-headed owl, unmistakable from any other.
2. Intense yellow eyes appear small in relation to the head and are surrounded by up to eight dark rings.
3. Ultradense, soft plumage provides excellent insulation against the cold.
4. Feeds on small rodents, birds, and occasionally frogs.
5. When viewed from the side, the head has a strange, flat-fronted shape.
6. In body size, largest of the noneared owls.
7. Soft grayish brown, cryptic plumage provides superb camouflage.
8. Most active hunting at dusk and dawn.
9. Females are up to a third larger than males.
10. Distributed throughout northern Europe, northern Asia, and extreme northern North America and subarctic Canada.

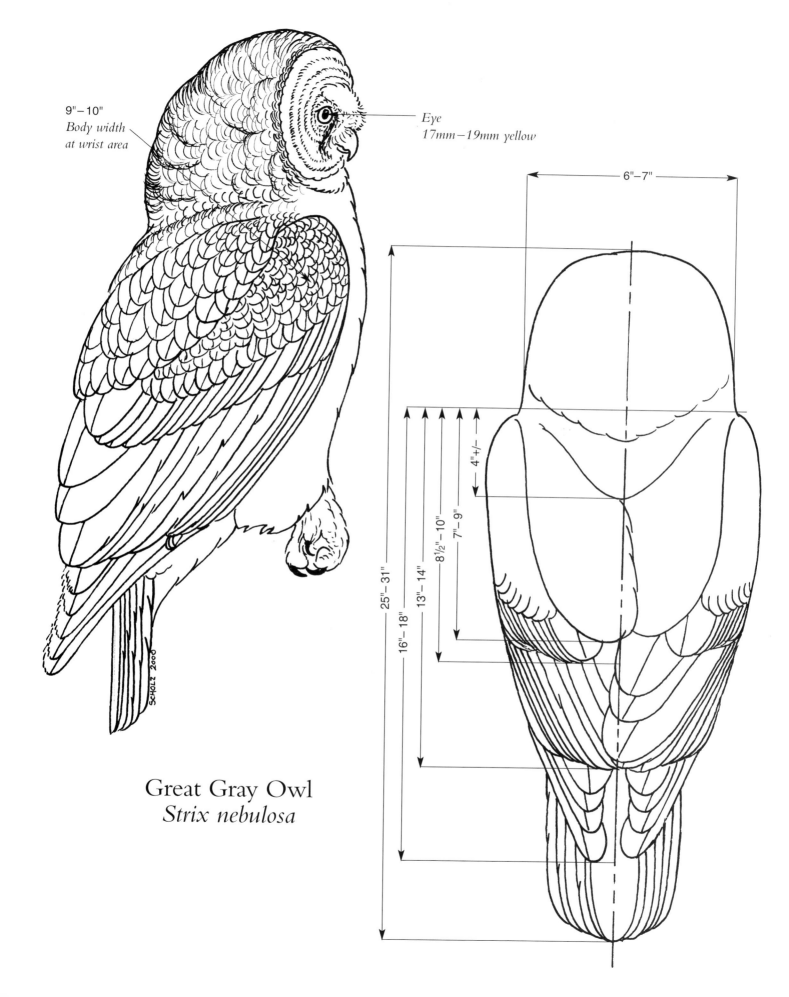

9"–10"
*Body width
at wrist area*

Eye
17mm–19mm yellow

6"–7"

4"+/–

7"–9"

8½"–10"

13"–14"

16"–18"

25"–31"

SCHOLZ 2000

Great Gray Owl
Strix nebulosa

The pure white bib gradually blends into the surrounding feathers as it extends outward.

The relatively flat-faced look is evident. Note the eye-to-beak proportion and prominence of the rictal bristles.

Intricate plumage patterns of the upper back corner of the head.

Note the eye placement, shape of the beak, and structure of the throat feathers as they cascade outward from the lower mandible.

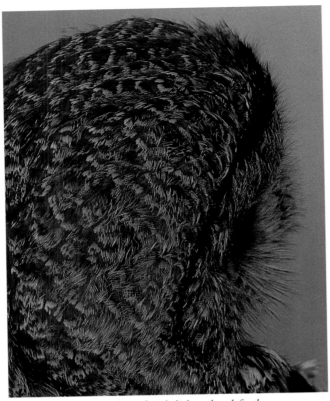

The transition zone from facial disk to head feathers.

A challenge for even the most skilled artist.

The unique herringbone structure of the facial disk feathers is clearly shown.

Opposite page: Notice the stiff, stubblelike eyelashes surrounding the eyelids.

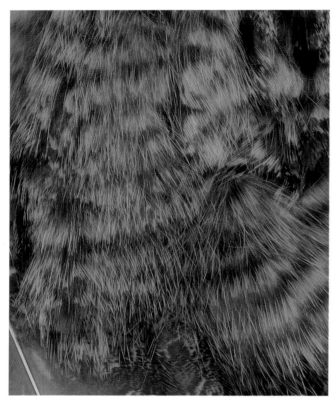

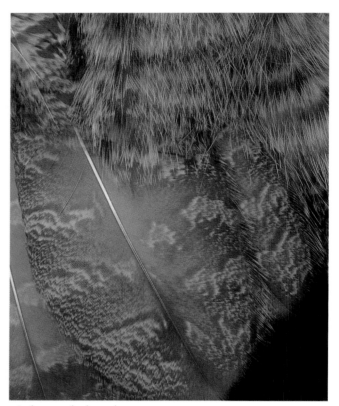

Lower belly feathering and the underside feather shaft of a flight feather.

A close-up look at the same area.

The underside of the secondary flight feathers is overlapped by the coverts.

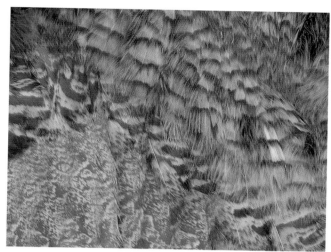

The feather structure changes dramatically from major flight feather to contour feather.

Note the soft breakup of the edges of these primary feathers. On the upper left, observe the fringes, which aid in silent flight.

The white throat feather structure.

The cryptic patterns found throughout the major feather groupings vary subtly as they shift from secondary to primary feathers.

The soft, cottony flow of the upper breast feathers just below the white throat region.

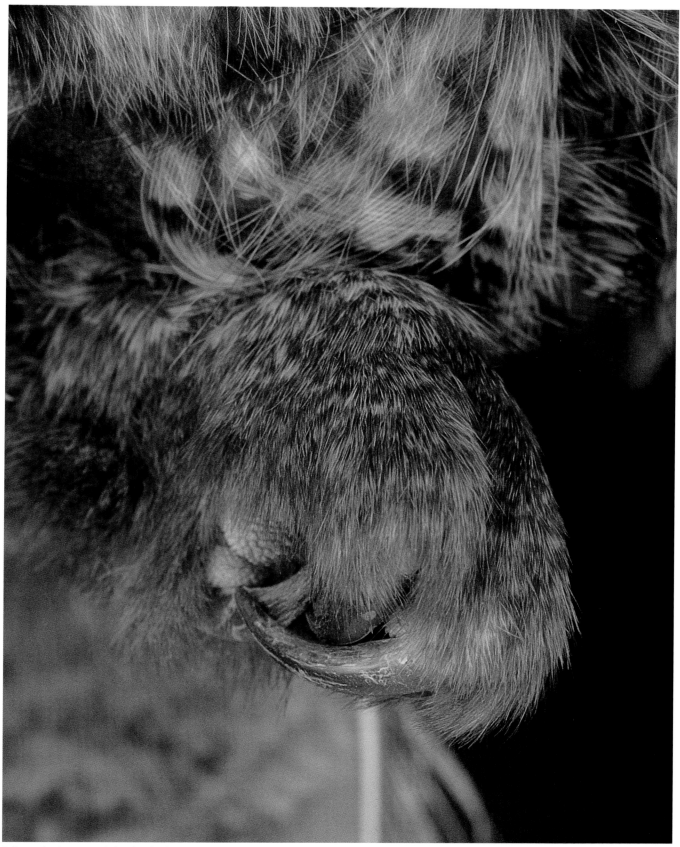

The right foot is tightly clenched. Great grays have extremely powerful feet tipped with long, needle-sharp talons. I'm always struck by the design of such a foot—how the formidable talons can fold so neatly together without puncturing the toe pads.

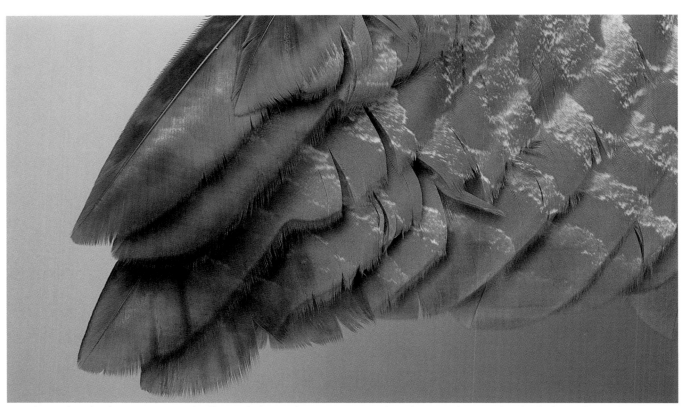

On the underside, the primaries gradually get darker and are quite pointed at the tips. This is a detail which can be easily overlooked when studying the feathers of the great gray owl.

Complex patterning and transitions in an upper wing section provide a kaleidoscope of changing textures, shapes, and colors.

An interesting variety of feather shape, texture, and color.

A partially open wing.

Feather size and shape shift abruptly coming off the primary and secondary feathers.

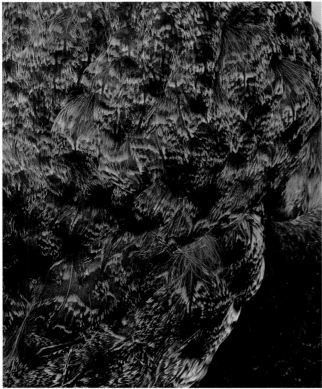

Gray and white vermiculations are interspersed with sienna tones on the back of the head.

The top tail feather, known as the deck feather, is centrally located. The pattern of the dark barring is much more defined than on a lot of other feathers.

The wing underside reveals secondary and primary flight feathers.

Opposite page: Underside barring of flight feathers.

The tertial feathers and lower scapulars.

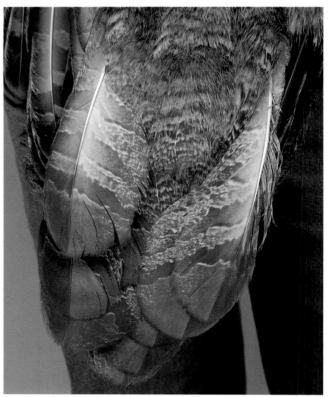

The long underside tail feathers and undertail coverts are revealed. Note the transition from almost pure silvery white to very dark tips.

Ever on the lookout for their next meal, these owls choose the highest perch around, typically the pinnacle of a tree.

RON AUSTING

This owl stretches its neck to get a better look at something that has caught its eye. It will then rely on not only its superb sight, but also its ultrasensitive hearing to locate the prey.

RON AUSTING

An adult great gray owl perches among the branches of a large cedar tree in northern Michigan.

RON AUSTING

The feet are all but invisible under the feathers covering this ghost of the North.

Opposite page: A view of a stately adult great gray owl as it blends into its environment. Great grays are masters of camouflage and surprise when hunting prey. RON AUSTING

Body posture shifts drastically as the owl is about to take flight in pursuit of its next meal. Up to two-thirds of the bird's weight is distributed directly above and in front of the legs.

Note the loose feathering as this great gray owl balances atop the thin branches of a spruce tree. Great grays possess a sense of balance which is almost unrivaled in the animal kingdom, allowing them to perch atop swaying branches.

RON AUSTING

Techniques for the Artist and Carver

ANY ARTISTIC ENDEAVOR MUST BEGIN WITH AN idea. Once a bird has been selected, it is up to you, the artist, to learn all you can about the chosen subject. There is no substitute for exhaustive research and tireless observation. Be a relentless detective in your pursuit of knowledge and understanding. Begin collecting information from every possible source, and force yourself to notice subtleties that others might not see. It's an artist's job to open the eyes of others, to stimulate curiosity and wonder, and to view things in a new way.

When carving, rely on your own good judgment and ability to "feel" the work in progress. There are no hard-and-fast rules, or definitive measurements, for establishing a pleasing composition. Books are available that give guidelines on tasteful and time-proven ideas about balance and harmony, but ultimately, the decision is yours. I have just three general pointers.

1. Always be sure that the center of focus is the bird. Everything else that is included should enhance the story or add to the composition.

2. Avoid clutter and the addition of unnecessary decoration that distracts the viewer's eye.

3. Try to make your sculpture interesting from all angles, avoiding, if possible, a "front."

DEMYSTIFYING COLOR THEORY: COLOR AND LIGHT FROM BLACK TO WHITE

To properly understand the elements of color, you must first understand the mechanics of light. Color perception and appreciation as we know it would not exist in an environment devoid of light. Recognition and comprehension of color is a direct result of incoming light waves stimulating millions of cone-shaped receptor cells concentrated on the back wall of the eye's retina. When color is seen, we are in fact only seeing the particular length of light wave from a color spectrum, which is reflected back to our eyes. All other colors are absorbed into the surface.

When viewed off a pure white background, the less complicated, or less "polluted" the color, the richer and purer the perceived color will be. It seems as more pigments are added into the original color mass, they intermingle and diminish the intensity and integrity of the reflected light waves.

When I'm in my studio painting one of my bird carvings, I try to avoid mixing more than three colors together to achieve a desired hue. Here's an experiment you can try: Mix together any five colors you can think of in equal parts and look at the resulting color. Chances are you will be staring at a mass of dull, muddy-colored paint, maybe usable for some type of marshy habitat but little else.

When painting your carvings, keep in mind that the plumage of most North American owl species is earth tone, ranging from soft browns to gray. When attempting to replicate the softness and richness of a bird's feathers, keep your color mixes as simple as possible.

After many years of teaching painting and color theory to bird carvers, I have come upon a basic system: By combining just two colors—burnt umber and ultramarine blue—with white, you can achieve an almost unlimited array of natural-looking earth-tone colors ranging from jet black to light blue-gray.

The real trick in painting the textured surface of a wooden bird carving with water-based acrylic paints is to apply the colors in thin, translucent wash coats over a carefully gessoed surface. Be absolutely certain that the previous layer is dry before applying the next coat, or it will lift and you'll have to start over. Above all, be patient. It may look like a patchy, blotchy mess at first, but after the forth or fifth wash coat, it will begin to even out. Avoid the temptation to thicken your paints to save time. This will result in an opaque, unnatural-looking surface—the exact opposite of your objective.

CARVING AND PAINTING HINTS AND TIPS

WHEN ROUGHING OUT

1. Always maintain your center line. If it gets sanded or carved away, redraw it immediately.
2. Base all of your measurements off that center line.
3. Maintain symmetry throughout the rough-out process. Absolute symmetry is essential in producing a lifelike and balanced carving.
4. Don't be afraid to draw on your carving.
5. Try to keep the surface of the wood as smooth as possible to allow for cleaner layout lines.
6. A good pair of wing dividers is helpful in maintaining symmetrical feather group layouts on each side of the body.
7. Proceed slowly. Exercise extreme caution when removing wood. It is always easier to remove wood than to try to add it after you have carved away too much.
8. Always be absolutely sure of your dimensions prior to cutting away any wood. The old axiom "measure twice, cut once" has particular relevance at this stage.
9. Always allow a little extra wood in the head and neck areas because subtle changes in attitude and posture are inevitable as the carving develops.
10. BE PATIENT.

FEATHERING, TEXTURING, AND PREPARATION FOR PAINTING

1. Rest work on a pillow while burning and sanding.
2. Use orthodontic elastic bands for holding sandpaper onto mandril.
3. Mist with alcohol prior to final sanding, then use 600-grit paper.
4. Use a polishing wheel for woodburner tips: rouge or white diamond work well.
5. An adjustable pedestal makes positioning work easier.
6. Use a mirror when setting and drilling out eyes.
7. Use a small fan to blow away burning smoke from the woodburner.
8. Use a small rubber sanding tube or the end of pencil eraser for contour sanding.
9. Sand extremely well in this sequence: 120, 320, 400, 600.

UNDERSTANDING COLOR

TERMS TO REMEMBER

Value: The lightness or darkness of a color when compared to a scale of grays (ranging from white to black).
Tint: Always used when lightening a color (adding white).
Shade: Always used when darkening a color (adding its complementary color or black).
Hue: The actual term used to describe true color.

PRIMARY COLORS
RED **YELLOW** **BLUE**

SECONDARY COLORS
ORANGE **VIOLET** **GREEN**

(Mix any two primary colors together.)

PAINTING WHITES

When painting whites to achieve softness and depth, think in terms of warm and cool instead of light and dark.

1. To warm up white, add a bit of red or orange.
2. To cool down white, add blue or violet.

When painting the carved and textured surface of a wooden bird, think of it as a landscaped surface. Warm the hills; cool the valleys.

ALWAYS PAINT FROM LIGHT TO DARK.

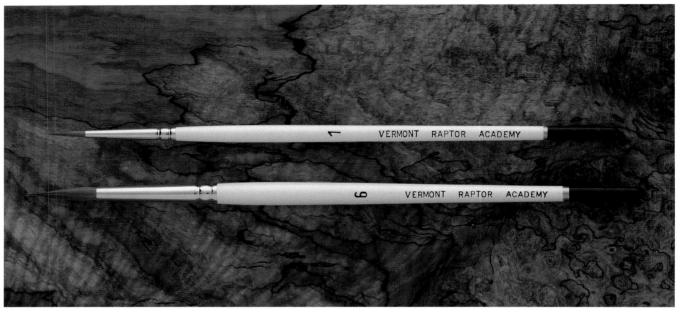

Excellent tools enable an artist to do excellent work. One area where you should not scrimp is with your brushes. These should be looked upon as an extension of your hand, and quality will give you maximum control and paint-holding capabilities. If you invest in good-quality brushes and take care of them, they will last a long time. When you are finished painting for the day, thoroughly rinse your brushes in clean, warm water. Then shampoo them and rinse again. Put a few drops of hair conditioner in a cup of warm water and swirl the brushes in this. Rinse them again, shape the bristles with your fingers to a perfect point, and set them aside to dry. This little bit of effort will yield huge benefits and protect your investment. The brushes pictured are available exclusively from the Vermont Raptor Academy.

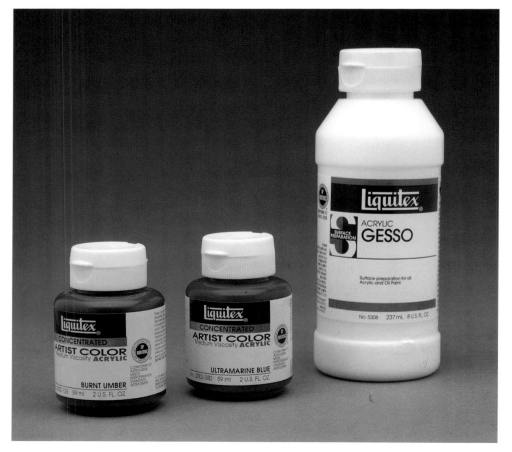

This is the magic combination. By mixing ultramarine blue, burnt umber, and gesso in different proportions, you can create an infinite variety of earth tones—browns, blues, and soft grays. These colors work for the vast majority of North American owl species, as well as rocks, branches, and other forms of habitat. Be aware that colors may vary among different manufacturers. Always experiment on a piece of scrap before applying a color to your project.

PROJECT 1 "FOREST GLOW"

When designing this pair of saw-whet owls, I wanted to tell a visual story. I placed the larger of the two owls (the female) in back of and above the smaller but more aggressive male. Saw-whet owls prefer to nest in deep, undisturbed woodlands—a habitat shared by white-tailed deer. To show evidence of this shared habitat and give the viewer an idea of location, I sculpted a small deer antler out of tupelo wood and perched the owls on it. The antler is grayed somewhat, from exposure to the winter elements, but it got hung up in a tree branch and so was spared from the busy teeth of rodents.

The base is heavily burled maple with a light amber stain to enhance the grain. The corners were stained lightly with a dark brown stain and allowed to fade into the center section of the post, creating an illusion of wooded depth. The overall height was critical to the success of the sculpture. If the birds were mounted too low on the base, it would appear squat and unpleasing to the eye. If the post were any taller, the sculpture would be visually top-heavy and unsettling to look at.

CARVING THE SAW-WHET OWLS

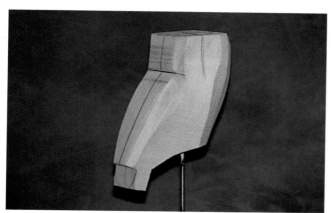

1 *Once the block of tupelo has been band sawed to a rough outline of the overall bird, the centerline is cleanly and clearly drawn in completely around the back, top, and front.*

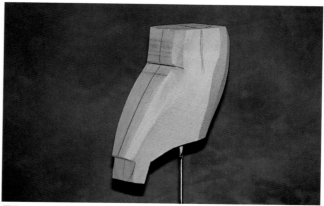

2 *The top-of-head centerline is established, and the front vertical centerline has been sketched in to aid in maintaining symmetry throughout the rough-out process.*

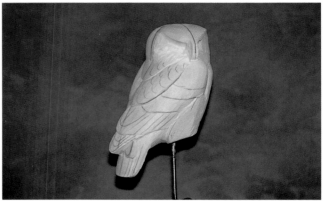

3 *Maintaining proper proportion and symmetry is essential in shaping the owl. All major feather groups have been blocked in, and head shape has been established.*

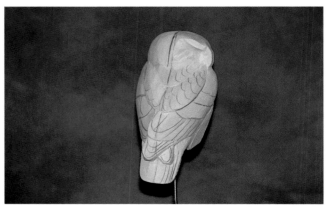

4 *Note the importance of redrawing the centerline to maintain balance.*

5 *Feather groups have been temporarily sketched in, and the eyes have been located and drilled out with a ¹/₂-inch wood-boring bit.*

6 *The beak and top of the head are shaped and sanded now.*

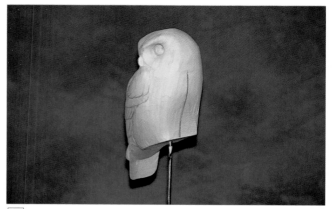

7 *Careful placement of the chest and belly centerline helps to correctly position these important areas.*

8 *More facial detailing around the beak is sculpted in. The tool used is a Gesswein with a pointed diamond bit run at 55,000 rpm.*

9 *Feather flow is laid out on the back of the head, and the final feather shapes and directional flow are drawn in the correct locations.*

10 *Using a ⅛-inch ruby ball mounted in a Gesswein tool run at 55,000 rpm, the contour feathering is outlined before stoning.*

11 *Deep contouring along the lower belly and flank feathers is sculpted into the wood using a #3 ruby flame (medium grit).*

12 *This view shows the opposite side of the owl, ready to contour stone.*

13 *The objective of contour stoning is to create a "landscaped" surface—definitely not texture. This process sets up and establishes all the "humps" and "bumps."*

14 *A good view of the completely contoured owl. The major flight feathers—tail, primaries, secondaries, and secondary coverts—are carved in with a tapered diamond cylinder (available through Jaymes Company).*

15 *The glass eyes are set into the sockets, which have been filled with A & B epoxy putty. A pencil eraser is a handy tool for positioning and focusing the eyes. (Hint: This epoxy has a working time of about an hour, so don't waste time when setting the eyes.)*

16 *The eyes are set at about a 45-degree angle to the head centerline. (They are angled much more than you might think.)*

17 *View of the other eye—ready for the eyelids.*

18 *You can give your bird quite a range of facial expressions, depending on how you set and sculpt the eyelids. A & B epoxy putty is used for this step.*

19 *Once the eyelids are formed, the owl is set aside overnight to let the putty harden. Then the bird is carefully sanded, first with 220-grit, then with 320-grit silicon carbide wet or dry sandpaper (available from 3M Company).*

20 *The outer facial disks are defined, and the white eyebrow region is carefully drawn in, based on reference photos and live bird studies.*

21 *The chest, breast, and belly regions are sanded with 600-grit silicon carbide sandpaper. They are now ready for final stoning detail.*

22 *The feather shafts are drawn in place. Then a wood burner is used to define and form the shafts. (Hint: Use a very low heat setting on your wood burner.)*

23 *The base is ready to accept the pretextured oil. The deer antler was carved from tupelo wood. The surface of the base was finished with three coats of semigloss polyurethane, sanded lightly with 600-grit paper between coats.*

24 *The lower portion of the saw-whet owl has been hollowed out with a small, round stump cutter to conform to the size and shape of the antler.*

25 *The second owl has been carved and added to the composition. (Hint: Carbon paper can be quite useful during the fitting process.)*

26 *A view of the composition from the front.*

27 *Two distinct personalities were my desire, so I set the eyes of the smaller male slightly closer together to give him an "angry" look.*

28 *I begin burning from the tail section and work my way up toward the head. A light, tight burn was my objective.*

29 *The wood burner is also useful for deepening and defining the rictal bristles in front of the eyes.*

30 *Here you can see the effectiveness of a good, tight contour burning technique along the upper wings.*

31 *All the contour feathers are carefully drawn in around the head before burning. This helps establish strong directional feather flow.*

32 *After the burning has been completed and the owls are carefully cleaned and inspected, they get two coats of a quality wood sealer before painting. (Once the sealer has been applied and dried, do not touch the carving.) Use a solid, well-made painting stick screwed up into the bird, and position the carving in a vise or other suitable holder.*

PAINTING THE SAW-WHET OWLS

1 *Once the carving has been carefully cleaned and sealed with one or two coats of a quality sealer, the gesso is applied. The objective is to achieve an overall consistency in coverage, allowing some of the burning shading to come through. The areas that are stoned for texture, such as the facial disks and belly areas, can be covered with a heavier application of gesso.*

2 *The gesso consistency should be like skim milk. Use water to thin the gesso, and add a drop or two of flow medium. Apply the gesso with a ¹/₂-inch oval wash brush.*

3 *Cover everything. Try to get the gesso into all the nooks and crannies. Once the owl is gessoed and ready for painting, do not touch the surface. Use a good, sturdy holding device.*

4 *A back view of the male saw-whet owl all gessoed and ready to receive the first of many wash coats of color.*

5 *A very thin mixture of 50 percent raw umber, 40 percent burnt umber, and 10 percent white was applied with a ¹/₂-inch oval wash brush, covering all the burned areas except the outer edge of the scapular feathers.*

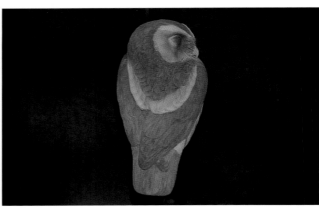

6 *A good view of the back region shows that a consistent brown tone is beginning to develop after about three wash coats.*

7 *The little male has been lightly airbrushed throughout the front areas to deepen the shadowing and show some three-dimensionality.*

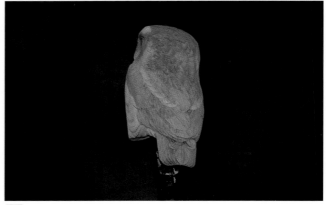

8 *The back of the male after four wash coats of the brown mixture.*

9 | *With each successive wash coat, the color deepens and becomes richer. At this stage, an airbrush can be used to deepen the areas in front of the eyes and accent parts of the facial disks and outside row of scapular feathers. (Note the delineation and depth of this feather group.)*

10 | *Frontal view showing the shade and shadow effect.*

11 | *The same back and base-tone color is used to airbrush the patterning around the facial disks and the soft brown streaking throughout the upper chest and flank areas.*

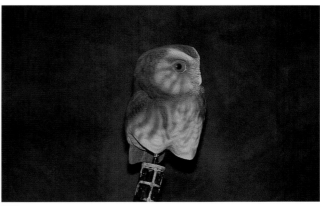

12 | *Side view of the head reveals the patterning and extent of the base-tone underpainting.*

13 | *Even at this early stage of the painting, a wide range of values is evident throughout the body.*

14 | *The same process is used on the slightly larger female owl.*

15 *Another view showing the pattern that radiates outward from its point of origin around the eyes.*

16 *Much detailing and tightening up of the different areas are accomplished with a #6 Vermont Raptor Academy sable brush. The lighter detailing was done with 60 percent gesso and 40 percent body color.*

17 *Very careful brushwork was used to highlight just the tops of the rictal bristles surrounding the beak.*

18 *When organizing and painting feather flow into and onto a broad area such as the chest and belly, establish a strategy and distinct pattern before committing yourself to the paint. This should have been carefully mapped out and sculpted during the carving process. This also holds true for the areas around the top and sides of the head.*

19 *The whitish streaks found throughout the head are a mixture of 70 percent gesso and 30 percent raw umber. The streaks lengthen as they flow away from the front of the head.*

20 *A view of the left side of the female owl. The light spots and bars throughout the body are added using a technique called scrubbing. Start with a small, soft brush (a #3, for example), cut the bristles down to within $1/8$ inch of the top of the ferrule, dip the tip of the brush in isopropyl alcohol, and lightly rub the areas where the spots or bars occur. This abrades the top layer of brown and exposes the white gesso underneath. (A word of caution: Don't overdo it. Rub away only enough to expose the white, or you will expose raw wood.)*

21 *Back view of the female shows that the edges of all the major flight feathers have been edged with the white mixture.*

22 *Particular attention should be given to areas with dramatic feather transition zones. In this photo, the soft side pocket feathers flow up and onto the upper wing.*

23 *Note the greater concentration of bright white spots on the forehead region. The fluff under the beak is highlighted by gently dry-brushing the tops of the feathers with the white mixture.*

24 *The right side of the smaller male as it nears completion. Lots of fine brushwork is essential to show the softness of these feathers.*

25 *The outer row of scapular feathers is "cleaned up," as is the white brow.*

26 *A close-up of the nearly completed male saw-whet owl. Notice the fine brushwork around the eyes and throughout the facial disks.*

27 *As an accent, burnt umber is used to paint individual hairlike lines throughout the chest and belly areas. Once the feet are attached, the remaining lower regions of the belly will be completed.*

28 *The owls are now permanently attached to the antler, and the little feet are glued into the body. A & B epoxy putty is used to blend the toes up into the belly.*

29 *Once the epoxy putty has hardened (about 12 hours), it can be lightly stoned for texture and then painted to blend with the surrounding areas.*

PROJECT 2
"MOONLIGHT OBSERVER"

IN CREATING A WINGED HUNTER AS POWERFUL and commanding as an adult great horned owl, certain compositional rules had to be followed. Simplicity and body position were my two overriding concerns as I worked to portray this patient, deadly observer of the forest. Technique dictated the carving, texturing, and painting of the block of wood, yielding an ultratight rendition of talons, soft feathers, and large luminous eyes. The owl sits up tall on a branch looking down on all it surveys, giving it an air of superiority and confidence. Its semirelaxed pose tells the viewer that this is a creature which fears very little. It is anchored by a 10-by 10-inch block of polished verde antique marble—

a haunting, dense representation of the owl's habitat. To add to the drama of the sculpture, the elevated owl is connected to its abstract base via a twister trident-based branch carved and painted to look like a bleaching assembly of bones.

During the process of carving I had to break off the primary feathers which overlap the tail to provide easier access to the carving, texturing, and painting of the upper tail surface. Breaking the wingtips left a jagged, uneven edge, which is much easier to conceal when regluing than if I had simply cut the wingtips off and reattached them along a straight line.

CARVING THE GREAT HORNED OWL

1 *The importance of drawing and maintaining a centerline when carving, especially while rough-shaping, cannot be overemphasized. Even at this early stage, the essence of the owl is projected.*

2 *The owl is placed on its back surface, revealing the care that goes into the contouring and feathering. In this photo, you can see how the side feathers flow over the wing area.*

347

3 *Despite the size of the workbench, it always seems to be cluttered. A number of special chisels and rotary cutters are used to sculpt the bird.*

4 *It's always helpful to have an expert on hand to make suggestions. My African gray parrot keeps a watchful eye on the evolving owl.*

5 *Dramatic sidelighting emphasizes the texture and contouring throughout the body of the bird. The feather shafts have already been put into the back and major flight feathers. A hydraulic power-arm vise is helpful in positioning the work, leaving both hands free.*

6 *If you look closely, you'll see that the primaries over the tail have been removed. This had to be done to carve, sand, texture, and paint the entire top of the tail area. Rather than cut them off, I just snapped them off. Snapping creates a jagged line that provides more surface area when regluing. The irregular glue joint also ties in more closely with the burning texture lines.*

7 *The eyes are now set in, and the eyelids have been formed. The best material for setting and sculpting the eyelids is A & B epoxy putty.*

8 *Very careful planning and layout were needed to pull off the throat and chin feathering. Two days of careful slicing with a surgeon's scalpel to remove fine wedges of wood were necessary to carve this fragile area. Notice the flow and rhythm of the upper chest and belly feathers and how they gradually increase in size as they flow downward. I refer to this as feather acceleration.*

9 *The mustachelike bristles that flow over and onto the beak are stoned in with a $^1/_{16}$-inch diamond ball. Then a wood burner is used to further deepen and clean up the region. Under the pineconelike chin feathers is a furry-looking group of throat feathers that will ultimately be painted pure white. A small white stone was used to texture this unique feather group.*

PAINTING THE GREAT HORNED OWL

1 *Once the carving has been thoroughly cleaned and sealed, it is gessoed white. Application of paint begins at the tail with a mixture of 70 percent burnt umber and 30 percent ultramarine blue. A #6 sable brush is used to paint in the dark markings on the tail feathers. Remember, do not touch the carving with your hands once the gesso has been applied. Despite washing, human hands are very oily and this could prevent proper paint adhesion.*

2 *The wavy ripples are emphasized by applying a slightly darker mixture very lightly into the ripples to accentuate them. This gives the collective feather group a lot more visual volume and makes it more exciting to look at.*

3 | *Using the earlier mixture of burnt umber and ultramarine blue, I continue to work my way up the wing region.*

4 | *There are absolutely no shortcuts to this operation. It takes a lot of patience and belief in your abilities.*

5 | *After about five days of nitpicking with a #6 brush, I've finally completed the head and face. The belly, breast, and feet are left. An airbrush can be very useful in painting shade and shadow on the front of the owl's body.*

6 | *Two weeks into the project, I'm making real progress with the belly and breast area. The branch sits atop a 9- by 9-inch solid block of Vermont verde antique marble. The branch is carved of basswood and reinforced with a ¼-inch-thick steel rod in the tall section.*

7 *As the great horned owl nears completion, my neighbor stops in to take a look. Don't be afraid to ask for honest opinions from people, even if they aren't experts. Despite your careful study and carving abilities, sometimes a fresh eye can pick up on something you overlooked.*

8 | *A close-up look at the completed great horned owl, "Moonlight Observer." I paid a lot of attention to areas such as the feet, eyes, and ear tufts. Typically, the number of feathers which make up an ear tuft group number from 5 to 7. In the carving process, it is sometimes easier and visually more effective to decrease the actual number of feathers. Otherwise, a blocky or built-up look may occur as a result of the wood's thickness.*

9 *A view of the overall sculpture. The verde antique marble is a very heavy, beautiful, deep green material.*

Gallery

"FOREST GLOW"

Northern saw-whet owl pair, 2000
Collection of Beatriz Scholz, Hancock, Vermont
Tupelo and acrylics with burled maple base

This enchanting pair of saw-whet owls was designed as a study in mood and personality. Huddled together atop the weathered antler of a white-tailed deer, the slightly smaller and more aggressive male shifts his weight forward to challenge an intruder.

As is the case with any artistic pursuit, the mastering of pure technique should be considered the foundation on which to build. It is only the starting point, from what must evolve an element of style and uniqueness.

With this in mind, I strove to make the faces of these two owls as distinctive as possible. This was a challenge, due to the small surface area. I accomplished this by slightly closing the eyes of the top female bird.

The late John Scheeler once told me that when it comes to bird carving, "the ability to transform a block of wood into a believable-looking bird is no longer

enough. Anybody can learn the basic skills necessary to accurately carve, texture, and paint a feather. The real test is to convey personality and feeling." This can be accomplished only through exhaustive and detailed research of the subject—not just its physical appearance, but also its habits and lifestyle.

The base is made of maple burl with a light walnut-colored stain on the corners, creating a nice variation in color saturation and depth. The platform subbase is red-wood burl. The color harmony of the birds, branch, and base works together in a balanced way.

A great deal of care was taken while painting the soft, furlike feathering of the chest, belly, and flank areas. Wonderful opportunities present themselves when you have a soft, light-colored mass of feathers overlapping a more distinct and darker area.

"MUSKEG MISSILE"

Northern hawk owl, 2000
Private collection
Tupelo and acrylics

Movement from behind has just caught the attention of this remarkable hunter. Excitement mounts as the body tenses in preparation for a possible aerial attack on its potential prey.

The northern hawk owl is a challenging bird to sculpt and paint. Because it is not commonly seen, the first obstacle is obtaining accurate reference material.

This bird seems to be assembled from parts of other birds. Its peregrine falcon–sized body is offset by a long tail and almost nonexistent, un-owl-like facial disks. Although on first examination you might see a dark, blackish brown body color, when you really study the colors, you notice a wide variety of brown values, along with shading, spotting, and distinct dark markings.

Six different values of brown were used to paint the back and head. To "juice up" the colors, I put a very light wash of deep magenta on the upper wrist areas and along the inner margins of the scapulars and nape. A great deal of detailed brushwork with a fine-quality #1 sable was necessary to achieve the softness surrounding the blazing yellow eyes. To portray the semi-gloss nature of the beak, I applied eight coats of thinned-out Elmer's wood glue with a touch of raw sienna acrylic paint and water. This gave me the color and depth I was looking for.

"REDWOOD FOREST RECLUSE"

Northern spotted owl, 1995
Private collection
Tupelo and acrylics

Deep, dark, dispassionate eyes seem to view the world from a unique and, at times, invisible vantage point. Northern spotted owls are truly one with their environment.

Artistically, my overriding thought when carving and painting this owl was softness. A number of combinations of burnt umber and ultramarine blue were washed over the body, creating an illusion of extreme softness. The lower belly feathers flow over the formi-dable feet and talons, making them almost disappear. The white spots were gradually intensified using gesso as a substitute for titanium white. A little bit of burnt umber was added to eliminate the starkness, as I didn't want the spots to be too bright.

To create an illusion of mottled feathering, I "hop-scotched" around the back area with a slightly darker wash of brown, deepening certain areas to create variety in color, tone, and depth. Also, notice how the spacing of the major flight feathers (tail, primaries, and secondaries) has been varied to create a realistic look. If all the feathers are laid out with exactly the same spacing, it can be boring—what I refer to as the "Venetian blind effect."

"MOONLIGHT OBSERVER"
Great horned owl, 1991
Private collection
Tupelo, basswood, and acrylics

Power and confidence are exuded by the "tiger of the air." Perched atop a gnarly dead branch, this owl shows off its deadly weaponry while its large, luminescent eyes survey every detail of its forest surroundings.

Artistically speaking, I pulled out all the stops to create a sculpture that personifies the power and majesty of this species. I perched the bird up high to give the viewer a sense of being looked down on. The branch, which is carved from basswood, flows down from the rapier-like talons to a sculpted tangle, out of which

three distinct branches offer support. All this is firmly mounted on a heavy block of polished verde antique marble, which is quarried near my home in central Vermont. The marble represents the lush Green Mountains, which provide the habitat for these great hunters.

Of particular note are the large, glowing eyes. I carved these out of ¾-inch-thick acrylic, creating a high dome to increase magnification. The yellow acrylic paint was mixed with something called an interference color (available from Liquitex). This addition created an iridescence that magnifies and subtly reflects light. When I delivered this work to the owner, I asked him to lower the lights, and the eyes glowed.

"SCREECH-OWL AND MOUSE"

1983
Collection of Drs. Myron and Karin Yanoff,
Philadelphia, Pennsylvania
Basswood, copper wire, and acrylics

This gray-phase screech-owl that has just caught a deer mouse was one of my first professional carvings. I strove to accentuate the predator-prey struggle within the confines of a circular composition. The body position of the mouse was critical, with the face hidden toward the rear of the piece. I didn't want the plight of the mouse to become the focus of the work.

I was experimenting with the use of acrylic paints, as up to that point, I had painted in oils. At first, it was an exercise in frustration, as I was attempting to work the acrylics as I would oils. Then, heeding the advice of my friend El Arnold of Cape Cod, I thinned the paints considerably with water. By painting wash coats in a watercolor approach, I was able to achieve some blending and softness, which has become the foundation of my style.

The pine branch was fabricated from copper wire, coat hanger wire, and dental floss. Habitat is a lot of fun to make and can enhance the sculpture and help tell the story. Try to avoid the temptation to add more "stuff" than is necessary to your base, as it will detract from the subject. How do you determine what is more than necessary? Observe, ask lots of questions, and rely on common sense.

"GREAT HORNED OWL AND BLUE JAY"

1985
Collection of Ron and Nancy Walborn,
Harrisburg, Pennsylvania
Tupelo and acrylics

This large, complex sculpture will always have a special place in my heart. It was the first major commission of my career, and it gave me a tremendous boost when I realized that I might be able to make a living doing what I loved most—bird carving. I would be hard-pressed to name another work whose design and execution took as much care and preplanning.

Compositionally, this sculpture is based around an equilateral triangle, which is one of the most stable shapes. Many of the great Renaissance artists were drawn to this shape. Not coincidentally, the subject

matter of many such artists had a religious theme. To Christians, the triangle has profound symbolism, representing the Father, the Son, and the Holy Ghost, and for this reason was to form the foundation of some of the greatest works known to man.

The French impressionist painter Paul Cézanne once remarked that when one looked to nature for artistic inspiration, the sphere, the cylinder, and the cone should provide all the underlying shapes on which to develop a composition. This suggests the existence of a harmonious relationship between people and nature.

A less-than-harmonious relationship occurs in my carving, as a rather irritated great horned owl is being scolded by a beautiful yet pesky blue jay. This scenario is one that happens all the time and often results in the powerful "tiger of the air" seeking a less visible and more peaceful location.

"BARN OWL"

1986

Collection of Michael and Marcia Kane,
Nantucket, Massachusetts

Tupelo and acrylics

Animation and accuracy were foremost in my mind when designing and carving this wonderful bird for a very special friend. This barn owl was my first attempt as a professional bird carver to open a wing and employ feather insertions throughout the body. I wanted to mount the owl on a spooky, gnarly, dark branch that flowed out of an old weathered base to convey a feeling of mystery.

Barn owls can be quite knock-kneed, and care must be taken to pose them with some semblance of balance and grace to avoid compositional clumsiness. Patience was needed during the painting process, as the plumage is a patchwork of ultrafine vermiculations, tiny spots, and subtle shading.

The dark eyes are set deep in the well-developed facial disks, which are framed by several rows of tight frills of feathers. I really had to do my homework to figure out the various feather groups and how they interact with one another when the body is twisted and the head is sharply turned.

"SOLSTICE"
Snowy owl, 2000
Private collection
Tupelo and acrylics

The solid, stable form of an equilateral triangle provides the compositional theme for this work. As hardened and resilient as the rocks on which it sits, the snowy owl is truly one with its environment. As a sculptor of birds in wood, I am continually striving for new and effective ways to convey a certain feeling or mood. When viewers are drawn to touch the hard, textured surface of the owl's body to convince themselves that what they see is not soft and yielding, I feel as though I've succeeded.

A sharp contrast exists between the gossamerlike plumage of the bird and the stark, forbidding rocks that form the base. The snowy owl and its base are all carved from one huge block of tupelo wood. My intent was to project as much sculptural integrity throughout the piece as possible by eliminating any add-ons and inserts.

Snowy owls are stocky, extremely powerful birds that have very little to fear, except for marauding polar bears. As far as predators go, this owl has certainly earned its place atop its rocky throne, surveying its unforgiving kingdom.

Seven months of carving and painting were needed to see this project through to completion. From a technical standpoint, I de-emphasized the texturing of the feathers, which allowed me much more painting freedom. Quite often, the structure and direction of the texturing have a direct effect on the placement and application of the paint. To convincingly paint the soft, dense, flowing plumage, I had to do a lot of brushwork. This would have been difficult if I were continually fighting against burned and stoned-in texturing.

Note the attitude of the legs. The left leg and foot are drawn up close to the body, and the right leg is extended downward, creating a connection between bird and base, between the animal and its environment. This uninterrupted flow provides an overriding unity to the whole work, allowing the eye to travel around the piece with little or no visual disruption.

"NIGHT WATCH"

Miniature great horned owl, 2000
Collection of Nancy Merrill, Rochester, Vermont
Tupelo and acrylics

The design and carving of a miniature bird can be every bit as difficult as creating a life-size one, if not more so. One must constantly be aware of proper scale and proportion. The most common mistake is making the head disproportionately large in relation to the body. This is sometimes done purposefully to amplify the Disneyesque cuteness of a smaller bird sculpture. In this scaled-down portrait of the great horned owl, however, I wanted to do a study of form and balance.

This owl has just settled onto a branch to begin a period of nocturnal watching and waiting. Great horned owls can sit motionless for hours on end, relying on their amazing cloak of virtual invisibility and ultra-sensitive eyesight and hearing to locate potential prey. Once prey is located, the mighty owl launches itself from its hidden platform and strikes on silent wings.

All the visual factors must be accounted for to present an attractive, well-balanced sculpture: size of the bird versus size and shape of the branch and base.

BIBLIOGRAPHY

Austing, G. Ronald, and John B. Holt, Jr. *The World of the Great Horned Owl.* New York: J. B. Lippincott, 1966.

Bent, Arthur Cleveland. *Life Histories of North American Birds of Prey*, 2 vols. New York: Dover Publications, 1961.

Cameron, Angus, and Peter Parnall. *The Night Watchers.* New York: Fourwinds Press, 1971.

Craighead, John J., and Frank C. Craighead, Jr. *Hawks, Owls, and Wildlife.* Harrisburg, Pa.: The Stackpole Company, 1956.

Forshaw, Joseph, ed. *Encyclopedia of Birds.* New York: Smithmark Publishers, 1991.

Hendrickson, John. *Raptors: Birds of Prey.* San Francisco: Chronicle Books, 1992.

Holmgren, Virginia C. *Owls in Folklore and Natural History.* Santa Barbara, Calif.: Capra Press, 1988.

Hosking, Eric. *Eric Hosking's Owls.* London: Pelham Books, 1982.

Hume, Rob. *Owls of the World.* London: Parkgate Books, 1997.

Johnsgard, Paul A. *North American Owls.* Washington, D.C.: Smithsonian Institute Press, 1988.

MacKenzie, John P. S. *Birds of the World: Birds of Prey.* Ashland, Wis.: Paper Birch Press, 1986.

Mansell, William. *North American Birds of Prey.* New York: William Morrow, 1980.

Parry, Gareth, and Rory Putman. *Birds of Prey.* New York: Simon and Schuster, 1979.

Perrins, Dr. Christopher M., and Dr. Alex L. A. Middleton, eds. *The Encyclopedia of Birds.* New York: Facts on File Publishing, 1985.

Quinton, Michael S. *Ghost of the Forest: The Great Grey Owl.* Flagstaff, Ariz.: Northland Publishers, 1988.

Read, Mike, and Jake Alisop. *The Barn Owl.* London: Blandford, 1994.

Richards, Alan. *Birds of Prey.* Philadelphia: Courage Books, 1998.

Rue, Leonard Lee. *Birds of Prey: A Portrait of the Animal World.* New York: Smithmark Publishers, 1994.

Soucy, Len. *New Jersey's Owls.* Millington, N.J.: The Raptor Trust, 2000.

Sprunt, Alexander, Jr. *North American Birds of Prey.* New York: Harper & Brothers, 1955.

Sutton, Patricia, and Clay Sutton. *How to Spot an Owl.* Shelburne, Vt.: Chapters Publishing, 1994.

Terres, John K. *The Audubon Society Encyclopedia of North American Birds.* New York: Alfred A. Knopf, 1980.

Toops, Connie. *The Enchanting Owl.* Stillwater, Minn.: Voyageur Press, 1990.

Walker, Lewis Wayne. *The Book of Owls.* Austin: University of Texas Press, 1993.

Weinstein, Krystyna. *Owls, Owls, Fantastic Fowls.* New York: Arco Publishing, 1985.

Whiting, Jeffrey. *Jeffrey Whiting's Owls of North America.* Clayton, Ontario: Heliconia Press, 1997.

THE VERMONT RAPTOR ACADEMY

The objective of the Vermont Raptor Academy is to promote and foster a better understanding and appreciation for the fine art of bird carving and bird art through comprehensive, in-depth technical instruction on all aspects of bird carving, painting, design, and composition. Students of all skill levels are welcome to participate in stimulating and challenging courses geared toward advancing the individual's carving abilities to the next level.

Attention to detail is the hallmark of a Vermont Raptor Academy seminar. Students come away pleasantly surprised at the amount of care, personal instruction, and attention they receive. To contact the academy, call 1-877-RAPTOR 5, or write to P.O. Box 150, Hancock, Vermont 05748.

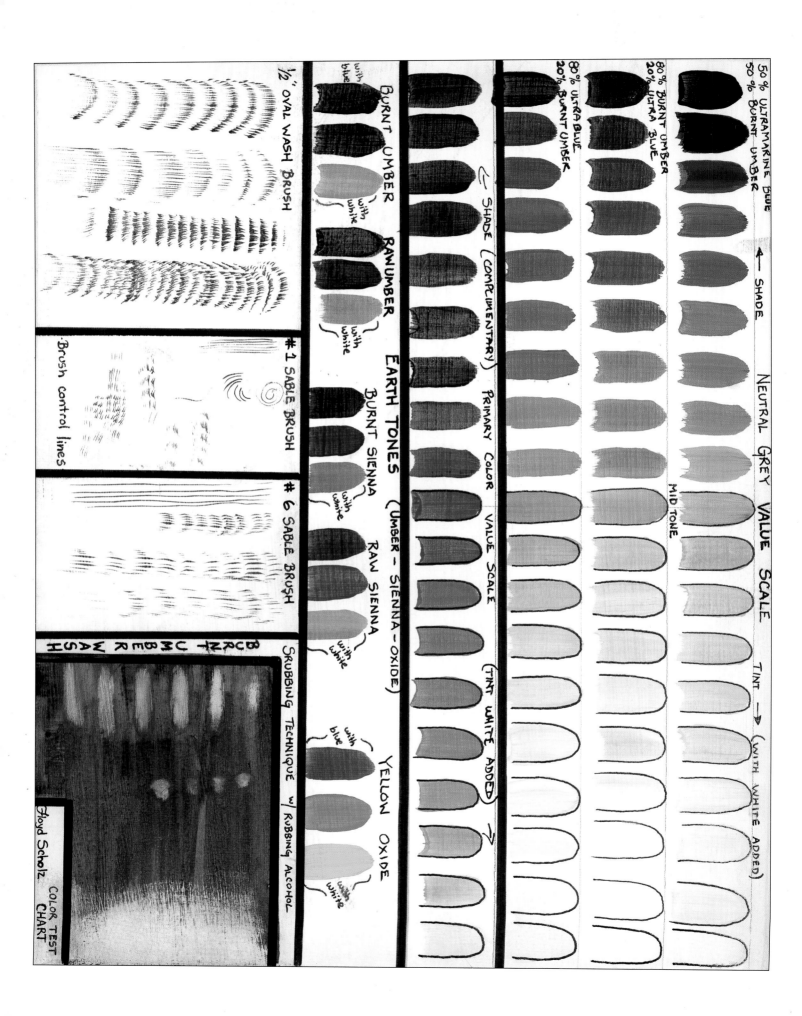

NEUTRAL GREY VALUE SCALE

50% ULTRAMARINE BLUE
50% BURNT UMBER

← SHADE   TINT → (WITH WHITE ADDED)

80% BURNT UMBER
20% ULTRA BLUE

80% ULTRA BLUE
20% BURNT UMBER

SHADE →

MID TONE

← SHADE (COMPLIMENTARY)   PRIMARY COLOR   VALUE SCALE   (TINT WHITE ADDED) →

BURNT UMBER

with white

with white

RAW UMBER

with white

EARTH TONES (UMBER ~ SIENNA ~ OXIDE)

BURNT SIENNA

with white

RAW SIENNA

with white

YELLOW OXIDE

with blue

with white

½" OVAL WASH BRUSH

Brush control lines

#1 SABLE BRUSH

#6 SABLE BRUSH

SCRUBBING TECHNIQUE w/ RUBBING ALCOHOL

B C
U R
R N
N T
T
U
M S
B I
E E
R N
R N
A
W A
A S
S H
H

Floyd Scholz

COLOR TEST CHART